# BE THE
# UNICORN

# BE THE UNICORN

## 12

### Data-Driven Habits That
### Separate the Best Leaders
### from the Rest

## WILLIAM
## VANDERBLOEMEN

HARPERCOLLINS
LEADERSHIP

AN IMPRINT OF HARPERCOLLINS

Published by HarperCollins Leadership, an imprint of HarperCollins Focus LLC.

Any internet addresses, phone numbers, or company or product information printed in this book are offered as a resource and are not intended in any way to be or to imply an endorsement by HarperCollins Leadership, nor does HarperCollins Leadership vouch for the existence, content, or services of these sites, phone numbers, companies, or products beyond the life of this book.

ISBN 978-1-4002-4711-0 (eBook)
ISBN 978-1-4002-4710-3 (HC)

Library of Congress Control Number: 2023943227

Printed in the United States of America

24 25 26 27 28  LBC  6 5 4 3 2

*For Adrienne:*
*the Unicorn who changed my life for Good*

# CONTENTS

# FOREWORD

Studying successful people doesn't always mean becoming successful. I can study the golf swing of Jack Nicklaus or Tiger Woods, and it won't turn me into them. Studying Michael Jordan's ability to slam dunk won't teach me how to slam dunk. Because some keys to success just cannot be learned.

But in this book, my friend William Vanderbloemen has not only studied successful people, he has unlocked the teachable habits they practice that make them successful. That means for you, this isn't just a book of case studies. You're holding a manual for becoming unusually successful—as unusual as a mythical unicorn. It's a manual based on hard data that unlocks the way you can become mythically valuable. Successful. Irreplaceable. He will teach you, as he puts it, how to become a Unicorn.

William's work lines up with and builds upon so much of what I've been teaching my entire career. And what's really compelling is that he's got the data to back it up. That's the remarkable thing about this book: more than thirty thousand top-caliber candidates and fifteen years of asking questions is what it took to get us here.

It's not surprising to me that curiosity is what led William to the conclusions found in this book. And it's not surprising that curiosity itself is one of the twelve traits that make a Unicorn. I am convinced that being curious and asking questions will take you on the most exciting journeys, so I encourage you to get curious. Ask yourself how you're going to develop yourself. Ask yourself in what ways you can grow yourself in these twelve areas.

Becoming a Unicorn won't happen overnight. And, like any other measure of success, becoming a Unicorn isn't a destination, it's a journey. It's going to take diligence and living in the present. It takes conscious and concerted effort every day. I've said it before, but every day we're either preparing or repairing. I encourage you to focus on what you can do each day to develop these twelve traits as you prepare to become a Unicorn.

I've said that everything good in life begins with a challenge, so this is my challenge to you: read this book, learn from this book, and live this book. Something magical happens when you commit yourself to personal transformation. And soon enough, you'll be a Unicorn.

—John C. Maxwell

# INTRODUCTION:
# THE RIGHT PERSON FOR THE JOB

**unicorn:** something that is highly desirable
but that is difficult to find or obtain

You can stand out in a crowd.

You can be the star.

You can be sought after and chosen, again and again.

You can be a Unicorn.

I know it sounds like a crazy promise. The world is filled with more humans than ever. For the first time in history, the workforce has five generations crowded in at the same time. In the age of hyperconnectivity and social media, everyone has a megaphone, everyone has a platform, and it's noisy out there. And with the dawn of a new era of artificial intelligence, I don't blame you for wondering when (not if) you will be replaced.

What I'm here to tell you is that you can stand out from your peers, and you can become irreplaceable. I've found a way to achieve this. It's based on data I've collected and studied over the course of my career. And I'm going to share it with you.

## WITNESSING THE X-FACTOR

Have you ever met someone, and within one or two minutes, you know that they're special? That they stand out from the crowd?

They are the energy in a room. They have a spark that lights up their environment. They don't seem to have trouble succeeding. And they seem to be the exception to the rules the rest of us are bound to. To me, they are like the unicorns that captured the imaginations of medieval Europeans. Unicorns were said to be magical. Simply being in the presence of one meant good fortune for all. Everyone wanted to be part of the Unicorn experience.

If you're like me, when you've met these people you've wondered if you could ever become that kind of person.

I've actually spent a lifetime trying to figure out what makes these modern-day Unicorns so special. I have discovered just what it takes, and what's more, I can teach it to you.

## Why me?

My name is William Vanderbloemen. I started and still run an executive search firm. I get paid to spot the best of the best. For the last fifteen years, very high-caliber organizations have tasked me and my team with finding their top talent. We aren't asked to "fill staff positions." We are asked to find the next superstar for our clients. The unusually talented. The effortless leaders. The irresistibly winsome. The Unicorns.

Today, with thousands of repetitions under my belt, I am pretty good at spotting Unicorns. I have seen them. Interviewed them. And I know more about them than ever before. In fact, I've not only learned how to spot them, but I've learned what qualities and habits they have in common. And I can teach them to you.

This isn't a book filled with my musings on what I think makes people likable or how I imagine you can stand out from the crowd. It's actually a how-to book for becoming one of those winning people, based on proven data. You see, I've spent the last several years studying the Unicorns I have met and learning what makes them tick.

*What makes a Unicorn?*

During the lockdowns of the pandemic, not many of our clients were hiring. In fact, nearly all of our clients were indefinitely closed (which I learned is not great for a small business . . . but that's another book). This slow period gave me time, and in that time I dropped back and began to seriously ask: "What makes a Unicorn a Unicorn?" "What causes these remarkable people to stand out?"

In a previous career as a pastor, I was always intrigued with the Unicorns. I would look for them in volunteers, in leaders, and in people I could learn from. The churches I served were filled with these kinds of people. What was most intriguing was how the Unicorns I came across came from every walk of life. I kept looking for common denominators, but I couldn't find them. Despite the inordinate value culture places on wealth and good looks, these weren't it. Neither was family status or level of education.

For each executive talent search we perform at Vanderbloemen, we put together a database of hundreds of candidates. That list of hundreds gets narrowed to dozens of exceptionally qualified people. That gets further narrowed to a handful of standout, Unicorn-level talents. Once we have identified that handful, we do a long-format interview with them. We have now done more than thirty thousand of those long-format interviews. My questions led me and our team to ask, "Who are the best of these thirty thousand interviews?" "How did they become the best, and who went on to truly succeed in their jobs?" Most importantly, we wanted to know if these Unicorns had anything in common.

We launched a massive study, not knowing if we would find any commonalities. The results of our study were at the same time stunningly congruent and shockingly teachable. Turns out, Unicorns don't share physical attributes. They weren't all good looking or tall or inherently athletic. What they had in common were traits and habits that were actually teachable.

A question I've asked throughout my life became a study. The results of a study became a guide for you, for anyone who wants to stand out from the crowd.

## LET'S INVADE FRANCE

People who stand out in work and life possess the power to get what they want and inspire others while doing so. I will give you plenty of examples in the coming pages, but a quick one to get us started is fictional, from the Apple TV show *Ted Lasso*. Team owner Rebecca Welton (played by Hannah Waddingham) is demonstrating to friend and mentee Keeley Jones (played by Juno Temple) how she makes herself feel powerful when she needs a boost of self-confidence. Keeley's reaction to her demonstration is a breathless, "You're amazing. Let's invade France." My mission in this book is to empower you with the skills to become an exceptional person who others watch with awe and inspiration in the same way that Keeley is awed and inspired by Rebecca.

After doing more than thirty thousand face-to-face interviews, I've started to see what those skills are. It turns out there are very clear ingredients for a successful person—twelve of them to be exact.

Yes, this book is the answer to the question I've been asking throughout my career. But this book is more than a book about talent and job searching. It's a book about distinguishing yourself from a crowded field and standing out as a Unicorn.

## DISCOVERING THE UNICORNS

If you want an insightful business book, get a preacher. (Said no one ever!) And yes, I come by my expertise via a long road that began with divinity school. Hardly the credentials one would expect, I admit. But hear me out. I maintain that what I've learned about people, particularly successful people, during my time as a pastor and throughout my life has taught me more than an MBA ever could. Don't get me wrong: There are brilliant business minds out there that I will never hold a candle to. But you don't need to have aced accounting to unite a roomful of people who can't agree on where to spend the endowment fund proceeds this year. You don't need to be Six Sigma trained to talk a grieving family through what they can expect at their loved one's funeral service. And determining who would be the best fit for the youth pastor position has so much more to do with your ability to read people than to read a spreadsheet. It's human skills that make the difference, not the formulas and algorithms that can be programmed. We've got machines for that, so why not let us humans do what we do best? My point is, when it comes to excelling, particularly in the workplace, it might be time to start looking for solutions in different places.

### The hard truth about soft skills

There is no profession that requires more excellence in soft skills and people skills than in my area of expertise, ministry and nonprofit work. Think about the last time you donated money to a nonprofit. Was it entirely because you believed in the cause? I'm willing to bet you had a charismatic standout from the organization aid in your decision. And how about the last wedding or funeral you attended?

On these days of great joy and of great pain, the pastor, rabbi, or other spiritual leader can make or break the experience for everyone. But the qualities we have identified in our own search efforts aren't limited to people who work in faith-based organizations. Soft skills are essential to success in any field or business and leaders of all types will benefit from the lessons that follow.

## Come with me if you want to live

Not to reveal my age, but *The Terminator* was a formative movie for me growing up, science fiction that now seems frighteningly close to reality. Machines may not take over the world, hunt down humans, and coin one of the most iconic catchphrases of all time, but they *are* taking jobs. And it appears that—with or without a cool motorcycle—they're only gaining speed.

Okay, maybe "come with me if you want to live" is a bit drastic. Let's say "come with me if you want to *thrive*." The truth is, experts predict that whole industries will be almost completely automated in as little as ten years. Health care, agriculture, and industrial sectors can all expect to be hit by an AI takeover. Of course, it's not all doom and gloom for us humans: the jobs we lose in these industries will be found in tech and robotics.

For better or worse, robots helped us out during the pandemic. When employers were scrambling to find labor that didn't get sick or spread infection, AI was there. As a result, economists estimate that 42 percent of jobs lost in the pandemic are not coming back.

Historically, we have feared innovation and tech advancements— but we've almost always been wrong to fear these things. I'm sure you've read some facts about humans' reaction to technology in times past that have made you chuckle. When we fret over technology "taking" our jobs or "replacing" us, we're being as foolish as the critics of the steam locomotive who were certain women's bodies could never safely travel at speeds as high as thirty miles per hour. The Luddites were wrong and so are we. AI isn't the apocalypse. It's an opportunity to evolve.

Bloomberg surmises that 120 million jobs are converting to AI, so for those 120 million displaced people, well, it's time to go back to school! And if not school, it's time to learn what machines can't. (Or can't *yet*.) While some jobs will go the way of the travel agent, it also means that there is tremendous job growth ahead and a chance for humans to redefine their value in the marketplace around the things AI cannot do. Most of that value? Soft skills.

After each of our thirty thousand interviews, I'd sit down with my team and highlight the best features from each candidate. Eventually, I began to see a pattern among the best of the best. What did the best interviews have in common? What did those people exhibit that made them stand out from the crowd? That's right: soft skills.

## *It's getting crowded in here*

Not only is tech taking jobs, but there are more workers than ever in the workplace. As I'm sitting down to write this book, we're coming out of the Great Resignation. Not to brag, but Vanderbloemen actually forecast this Great Resignation before anybody else. We saw it coming and now we're seeing what happens next. Soon most of those who left work are going to want to find work. Maybe even return to their previous work. And when that day comes, people have to stand out from the crowd like never before.

So what would it look like to up your soft skills? What would it look like to be one of those people who stood out in the crowd? The interesting thing that we discovered about soft skills is that every one of these skills can be developed or improved upon.

Olympic sprinters are fast. And most of us can never train to become as fast as they are. As much as I'd like to win the NBA slam dunk contest, I'm fairly certain a five-foot-nine person with average jumping ability is just not going to win that contest. Not all of us can become exceptional in certain skills. But we can get better and reach our own highest potential.

The Unicorns hold a skill set that can be learned. What we've discovered in our research is that these people have skills that can be developed by anyone.

That's why I'm so excited about this book. The day is coming when interviewing is going to be less about competence and more about soft skills and cultural fit.

## SOFT SKILLS WIN

I'm always amazed at how, when we do a search, and we get down to two finalists, the person who wins the job is simply, as one of my senior consultants says, the person who plays best with others.

I hope you'll take time to read this book slowly. I've tried to build in descriptors of each of the soft skills that we've noticed among the Unicorns. But I've also left room for questions at the end. This book isn't just a narrative, and it isn't just a science study. Hopefully it's a manual. Hopefully it's a guidebook you can follow to become one of those people who stands out in the crowd.

It's a brave new world out there, and standing out is more important than ever. The good news is that doing so is within your reach. Let's take a journey together and learn from the Unicorns. It may just change your life for good.

# BE THE UNICORN

# ONE

# THE FAST

Blake Mycoskie doesn't miss a beat. Throughout his life, Mycoskie has let speed guide him, propelling him from one opportunity to the next. When an injury ended his college tennis career, Mycoskie left school and started a successful laundry business. Then he moved to Nashville and started a media company. Mycoskie Media succeeded even faster than EZ Laundry. Having bounded from one success to the next, Mycoskie and his sister teamed up on the second season of *The Amazing Race*, which, it seems to me, is pretty on brand for the hustling entrepreneur. Everything Mycoskie does, he does with speed. More opportunities and successes followed, and in 2006, Mycoskie started what we now know as Toms shoes, which is one of the earliest and most successful examples of social entrepreneurship. Not content to slow down, present-day Mycoskie is still investigating new enterprises, still racing to find the next big thing for himself, sure, but with a sharp focus on what his next endeavor can do for the world.

We've all been told to play it cool at some point in our lives. Don't accept the first offer; wait a few days before returning the call/text/whatever of a potential suitor; cast and then let the fish have a little time with the lure before reeling back in. Looking overeager weakens your position, right? Wrong.

Speed wins.

Unicorns know this. For as many aphorisms there are warning you not to move too fast, there are still more urging you to fling wide the door the moment opportunity knocks. We live in a time of on-demand everything. If we ourselves are not on demand in some capacity as well, we lose. We lose opportunities to achieve more and be more. Response time matters.

## WHAT WE KNOW

Okay, so "be responsive." Is that it? That's it. While this seems like an easy one to hack—and indeed is the easiest of the twelve traits—it's harder than it sounds. Acting fast isn't always in our nature, especially when we're afraid.

### Being fast is scary

"He was a bold man that first ate an oyster," wrote Jonathan Swift. Being fast is often associated with being first, and being first comes with a lot of risks. It's much more comfortable for us to wait and see what happens to the first guy before we act on an opportunity of which we're unsure. Uncertainty is hard on our brains. After all, they evolved with the express purpose of keeping us alive and well. Our brains are vigilant, always trying to guess what's going to happen next so our bodies can be ready to react in a way that keeps us safe. When we don't know what's coming next, we can't plan. When we can't plan, we could die. (Admittedly, this was much truer for our ancestors venturing out of the cave in the dark of night, but some habits aren't easily shaken. It's hard to prove a negative; we can't always convince our brain that we're *not* going to get eaten by a saber-toothed tiger.) In our early days as a species, it made a lot of sense to wait for another person to leave the cave first. And to this day, our brains are doing the work to keep us from harm. When the boss asks the group for "honest opinions," your brain tells you to let Jim from HR go first so you can plan your answer accordingly.

Our brains are also predisposed to procrastination, but for slightly fewer noble reasons than "keeping this person alive." That's because our limbic system (the brain's pleasure center—woo, party!) is much stronger than our prefrontal cortex (the planning part of our brain) and tends to win. The task can wait till tomorrow.

**Fast fact:** The word *procrastinate* comes from the Latin *crastina*, which literally means "tomorrow."

## *Being fast doesn't mean saying yes*

There's a lot of evolution and neuroscience to learn and unlearn on the path to becoming the Fast. But it's important to remember that being fast doesn't mean saying yes to everything always. Rather, it means discerning (quickly!) what needs an immediate response and what does not.

In the start-up world, there's a cautionary phrase: beware of distractions disguised as opportunities. It can take a lot of discipline, plus some trial and error, to teach yourself the difference between distraction and opportunity, but the more you practice the better you get. I'll give you some tips for telling what's what at the end of this chapter.

*The risks are worth it (usually)*

I run. More accurately, I jog. I do this for all the usual reasons: it clears my head, it boosts my energy levels, and I've never met a piece of fitness tech I haven't wanted to take out for a spin. Over the years, I have found the best predictor of me actually going for a run on any given day is if I do so at the first chance I get. When I tell myself I'll do it later, later rarely comes. I sit down, start scrolling through social media, and that's the ball game: another check in the "win" column for the limbic system.

Being able to quiet the limbic system—with its lies about taking a run after work and entreaties to see if there are any donuts in the break room—and doing now what you probably won't do later is the best choice and the preferred practice of Unicorns.

We have an impulse to act fast when we are excited about an opportunity that we think will benefit us. No need to wait for HR Jim to go first in this case! How many times has this happened to you? You fell in love with some product in some store. Maybe it's the pair of shoes you knew you were born to have. Maybe it was the watch you've been searching for your whole life. Or maybe it's the latest high-draw driver with the Fujikura shaft that will 100 percent for sure put you on track to join the senior tour when you retire from corporate life. It doesn't matter what the product is. You love it, you want it, you'll buy it today. You hand over your credit card and tell the sales associate to box it up. And then they break your heart: The product you're looking at is for display only. And they're out of stock. You'll have to wait two to three days for another one to come in. Should they process your card now and give you a call when it comes in?

No. The spell has been broken long enough for the prefrontal cortex to kick in with all the reasons the purchase is a bad idea. The item has lost its luster, and suddenly it's just another Saturday at the mall. Your limbic system suggests going to Cinnabon.

*There is no time like the present*

Salespeople know better than anyone how important response time is. If you aren't there for your client *now*, you may as well not bother.

The data is here to back this up. A 2021 study looked at over 5.7 million inbound leads and determined which were most likely to convert. The answer: the ones a rep responded to in *less than five minutes*. If those leads weren't attended to in the first five minutes, the chances of them converting plummeted by a factor of eight.

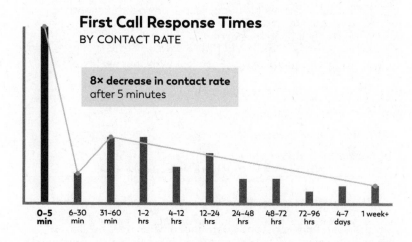

Five minutes is all it takes to miss out on a lot of potential revenue. It makes you wince, doesn't it? The good news is, we know how to prevent this kind of revenue exodus. The mind boggling news is, so few people actually take action to do so. But not you. Not anymore. You're becoming the Fast.

### WHY HIRING MANAGERS LOVE THE FAST

The Fast are a hiring manager's *dream*. The Fast respond quickly so they can proceed with next steps. There's no dithering: any hardball that's being played will be played quickly and efficiently. The Fast will get their paperwork in on time. The Fast will be the ones to get the interview and then the offer.

**Tips to cultivate Fast practices at work:**

- Make it clear that quick response time is a company value.
- Offer incentives for faster responses.
- Set quick, achievable deadlines; no one needs a month to make their benefits elections.
- Try the Vanderbloemen Fast Test with your next hire.

### WHO IS FAST? LIN-MANUEL MIRANDA

The *Hamilton* creator and star is the best example I know of the Fast. I am constantly astounded when he is on Jimmy Fallon and does the "Wheel of Freestyle"—a bit where he gets three random words and then immediately produces a freestyle rap containing all three words. It's obvious he's a genius and that genius is at least partially to do with his gift of speed. Lin-Manuel Miranda not only thinks fast, he acts fast as well. For years, including while he was onstage in *Hamilton* up to eight times a week, he tweeted thoughtful, not ponderous, thoughts of love and encouragement morning and night. Immediately after Hurricane Maria, he sprang into action to help the people of Puerto Rico. Lin-Manuel Miranda doesn't appear to overthink things. Rather, he trusts himself to do what's right or what will work and then he does it.

## WHAT WE'VE SEEN

In business and relationships, being quick to respond almost always pays off.

When I was a young senior pastor, we were looking for a new place to hold worship while we were waiting for our new space to be built. One of the elders in the church took me driving around to look for a location. Right across the street from the property we had purchased to build on was a YMCA that was not being used on Sunday mornings.

The board member said to me, "I think I know the chair of the board of the YMCA. Here's his phone number. You could call him and see if we could use the facility on Sunday mornings."

I thanked him and began to talk about another subject. When we were back in the office, he listened to me talk to some colleagues for a minute or two and stopped me. He looked me in the eyes and asked, "When are you going to call the chair of the board of the YMCA?"

"I'll get around to it pretty soon," I said. To be honest, I was a little annoyed. I'd taken the number and said I was going to make the call. He didn't need to micromanage me. This "opportunity" felt way more like a distraction.

His response? "Why don't you call him right now?" He went on to say, "I've learned that if I have time to take care of something right away, it usually is the best time to get things done."

He was right, of course. And since then, I've seen time and again how candidates who are fast and responsive are candidates who act quickly and get things done.

### Fast is a great indicator of success

In our experience at Vanderbloemen, the candidates we reach out to are very slow to respond. Normal response time for these types of leads is over two days. Normal response time from candidates who are (a) already on our radar and in our network, (b) have expressed an interest in finding a new job, and (c) have actively entered a search is still slow, usually around a business day.

When we reach out to a candidate via text, email, phone, or LinkedIn, if we receive a response within a minute, it still turns heads in the office.

Fewer than 1 percent of candidates respond within a minute.

Those candidates who respond within a minute get fast-tracked. Not coincidentally, our experience is that the 1 percent who respond immediately to a text have stayed the longest at their placements—indicating job satisfaction—and have been rated as "highly valuable" by their colleagues.

*Being on the receiving end of Fast: the Vanderbloemen Text Test*

With speed, the medium is the message. The overwhelming evidence shows that texting is the fastest way to a prospect's heart—or, at least, consciousness. Most text messages are opened within three minutes. And with the ease of use that accompanies them, most are responded to quickly as well.

At Vanderbloemen, we use this data as another way to discover if a candidate is right for us. Some may call it "borderline entrapment," but we like to refer to it as "putting our values into real-life situations and seeing what happens." Here's our not-so-secret "text test."

When we're vetting a new candidate, there's a significant chance they'll get a text message from someone on our team—and not necessarily the person who interviewed them—but someone they talked to here at some point. They'll likely get the text at a late-night hour, maybe around 10:30 p.m. The message will probably be some kind of weird question such as, "Okay, the Astros have won over fifty games before the All-Star break. How many teams that do that also win the World Series? Do you know?"

If they don't answer, it doesn't mean they'll lose the job. But if they answer within the first minute, saying, "Ha ha, I love the Astros too," then they'll get a big-time bonus point (for loving the Astros) and another point for answering within one minute, which aligns with the idea of ridiculous responsiveness. If they answer with something like, "Well, I looked it up and only three teams have done that. The Rangers did it twice and the Astros once. The Astros blew the World Series, and the Rangers won it both times," then I know (a) they're ridiculously responsive, (b) they've made me go "Wow!," (c) they've shown solution-side living, and (d) they've shown contagious fun because they're snarky about the Astros, which is fine by us!

It sounds simple, responding to a late-night text, but it's very telling for our recruiters. I have, however, ruined this part of the test now because I've told the story . . .

We don't tell people these little tests are part of the interview. If they pass the test, we tell them, "Look, we have communication guidelines during off-hours. It's not a free-for-all text 24-7, but if you get an email, answer us the next time you're on your computer, within twenty-four hours. If you get a text after hours, answer it right away. If you get a call, pick it up. If that's going to make you crazy, then we want to test for that right away."

The text test is one of the best and easiest tools we have to predict a candidate's success.

### Report from the Unicorns

When we sent our survey to our database of Unicorns, only 2.6 percent identified "fast" as their best quality. Still, I uncovered a lot from this 2.6 percent that informs what goes on inside the minds of the Fast.

It shouldn't surprise anyone that a lot of the Fast attribute their speed to a military background where being fast is often a matter of life and death. They've brought that urgency home with them, to use in their personal lives as well as the workplace.

Timothy C. tells us: "I'm fast thanks to my military and army aviation background. Both require a rapid assessment of the situation and quick decision-making skills. In combat or flying, this is a required skill for successful outcomes."

"Make a decision!" says Patrice M. "Quickly gather the information necessary to make a decision, knowing that we will never have all; we'll never know everything. Be decisive. Commit and move forward. The unwillingness to commit, combined with a fear of failure, paralyzes many in positions of leadership. No, not every decision will be a good one, but fail fast and learn."

"By serving in the US Navy for eleven years and rising to the rank of chief petty officer, I learned to be accurate but also fast enough to pump out lots of work in short amounts of time while utilizing all the men serving under me," says Jack J. "I worked by making lists at the end of each day that had to be done the next day, week, month, etc., and cross-checked it with manual requirements to generate lists for each of the men, myself included. I would go back over the checklists to make sure all work was completed accurately and efficiently. I still do this in my career today."

## WHAT WE DO

Some of the Fast come naturally to the habit of rapid response. The rest of us have to hone this skill our whole lives.

When you're born with it, you know. And even before *you* know, your parents know. My wife and I are both very quick to respond and quick to act. We've had one child together. Everyone wondered what would happen when William and Adrienne's genes are mixed. What happened was our daughter, Macy.

Macy was just beginning to talk. But instead of having a first word, she had a first sentence. One morning, she was bouncing in one of those bouncy seats the toddlers play in and looked across the room at a toy she wanted. She looked back at me and said: "Do it!"

I laughed and got her her toy. I guess Nike's "Just do it" slogan was too long for Macy? She was a girl on a mission and keeping the "just" clearly took too much time. Ever since then, she's shown an uncanny quickness to respond.

If you don't have nature and nurture working for you like Macy has, don't worry. We can help you get so good at being the Fast that EMS services will want to take master classes from you.

*Here's how*

In golf, speed is all the rage right now. There's a lot to be said for mass, but speed is having its day. If you want your ball to go far out of the tee box, maximize the force you're putting on that ball. To achieve this, designers and physicists are coming up with new and creative ways to optimize your clubhead speed.

**Fun fact with serious implications:** For every one mile per hour of speed you add to your golf swing, you will gain more than three yards of distance.

In our own bodies, athletic trainers remind us that we have to work on speed, or it will naturally decrease with age. Speed is a "use it or lose it" part of our lives. If you don't practice moving fast, you can kiss it goodbye. The same is true for response time in your day-to-day life.

*Speed barriers . . . and how to break them*

Two things can keep you from living up to your potential as a member of the Fast:

1. Access to the opportunity
2. Fear

Access: You can't respond quickly if you never receive the message. Maybe your phone is charging in the other room, maybe you never check your email, or perhaps your only digital presence is a MySpace account you set up in 2004. Now, we're not saying you need to be everything everywhere, all access all the time, but you do need to allow for messages and opportunities to find you in the first place. While they're not necessarily my thing, happy mediums do exist. If you don't think you can respond quickly to a call, text, or email, set up an autoresponder. You can have your "you" time without it costing an opportunity.

Sometimes the opportunity is right there. It has found you. Maybe you heard the text come through or maybe you're sitting in an audience of a magic show and the magician is pointing straight at you. That's when fear comes in.

Like I said before, being the Fast is not a matter of saying yes to everything (the magician will just have to get someone else to cut in half, thanks very much). It's a matter of determining what your answer should be quickly. Fear can paralyze your decision-making.

Questions to consider for the fastest possible response time:

Is this a distraction or an opportunity? I told you I'd be back with some tips for determining which is which! Check out this chart the next time you're not sure:

| DISTRACTION | OPPORTUNITY |
| --- | --- |
| Doesn't get you closer to your goals | Gets you closer to your goals |
| Your limbic system gives it a "heck yes." | Your whole brain agrees on it. |
| Takes more time/money/resources than it is worth | Yields results that are worth the sacrifices you have to make for it |

Are you overthinking it? Fear *loves* to make you overthink. Overthinking makes you safer, right? You're more likely to get the right answer or work out all the possible scenarios if you overthink. "Thinking" is valuable. Overthinking is not. Some of my favorite people are overthinkers. The work they do is studied and flawless. They put so much care into how their audience will interpret their response. Unfortunately, the beautifully crafted email they send three days later is of no use when you needed a yes or no within the hour on the first day.

Are you overthinking? Some questions to ask yourself:

- Am I responding to a head of state? Will my response need to be unimpeachable? Most of us take things at face value. Frankly, most of us aren't big enough deals to warrant the Perfect Response. Good grammar and spelling are important, but if you're waiting to get a three-sentence text message vetted by the copy chief of the *New York Times*, stop and send it as is. You're fine.
- Is the time I'm spending on this response even remotely proportional to the level of importance this has?
- Am I overthinking this? If you have to ask, yes, yes you are.
- Is this an irreversible action that can have ramifications for my family generations into the future? Or is it just your lunch order?
- Am I being wise or am I afraid? There is a time and a place for responding slowly. (William Congreve's "Marry in haste, repent at leisure" comes to mind.) But those times and places are few and far between. Respond now and move on to the next opportunity.

*Speed comes from confidence*

Michelle L. tells us that confidence is key to a fast reaction time. "I was raised by a single mom. She gave us chores to do and a deadline on when to get them done. No micromanagement. We made decisions along the way. This gave us confidence with getting things done. As a leader, I get adequate information about a problem and make the decision without second-guessing myself. No need for perfection. Sometimes you fail but you learn and keep moving. There is not much that you can't recover from."

## FAST TAKEAWAYS

- Our brains don't always want us to be fast.
- We need to learn when to act fast.
- Quick response time in business and relationships is almost always beneficial.
- A new driver won't necessarily fix your golf game. But it could.
- Practice speed.

# TWO

## THE AUTHENTIC

**CASE STUDY: THE AUTHENTIC UNICORN**

Warren Buffett is the archetype for authentic leadership, with enough quotable quotes on the subject to fill Kiewit Plaza. Among these: "It takes twenty years to build a reputation and five minutes to ruin it. If you think about that you'll do things differently." Buffett became who he is—at this printing, the fifth wealthiest person in the world—in part thanks to strict adherence to authenticity. He has spoken and written time and again on the importance of owning mistakes. (Though, as one of his more famous quotes goes, it's preferable to learn from others' mistakes.) Great leaders, says Warren Buffett, are willing "to confess mistakes and invite others to do the same." For someone who can more than afford to project any image he wants, Buffett has found success, peace, and vocation by being exactly who he is.

Living in the Google era means there is no hiding. Whatever secrets you have will be discovered. The delivery (or lack thereof) on whatever promises you make will be found out. Authenticity is quickly becoming a differentiator between the best candidates for jobs and the rest. So what are the ways to develop your own authentic and transparent self while maintaining your sanity and privacy?

This chapter will show you how to build transparency and trust, and explain why that will help you stand out.

## WHAT WE KNOW

"I'm so much cooler online." The words to that old country song are truer than ever. Pictures are polished. Reality is spun. With endless Instagram filters, software, and an isolated world, it's just a lot easier to look better online than you really are. But those who can develop the ability to be authentic in their work and in how they present themselves are both rare and in high demand.

> **Authentic fact:** It's estimated that 80 percent of people lie on their online dating profile. Be careful out there!

### *Fake it till you make it, or not*

As Derek Thompson of the *Atlantic* pointed out: if you woke up on a Casper mattress, worked out with a Peloton, Ubered to a WeWork, ordered on DoorDash for lunch, took a Lyft home, and ordered dinner through Postmates only to realize your partner had already started on a Blue Apron meal, your household had, in one day, interacted with eight unprofitable companies that collectively lost about $15 billion in one year.

It's as if for the last decade we have invested billions in companies—and people—that aren't authentic at all. Companies that could talk a good game and sound like a good idea were valued, even if they weren't actually worth what they said they were. We rode that wave, and then we followed it to the documentaries and films that it produced: *We Crashed, Inventing Anna, The Dropout.*

What can I say? People love meteoric rises to fame and the crashes that can ensue.

Flash and dazzle are great for sprints, but if you want to win the marathon, you're going to need authenticity.

## Why we gravitate toward the authentic

We are afraid of authenticity because we live in a culture that looks ah-*mah*-zing! We polish and buff and filter our way into looking like model (literally) versions of ourselves when we share anything online. Why would anyone want to share anything that's not their best?

That may hold true for us individually, but the culture is shifting, and you've probably noticed it if you spend any amount of time on social media. Suddenly we're seeing "real people" demonstrate and review products that are being advertised to us. It's called user-generated content (UGC), and it can be defined as any Average Joe posting a review or a demo or an unboxing of a product or service.

These Average Janes and Joes look just like us as they apply the latest color correcting makeup or switch their traditional T-shirts to ones that work for "dad bods." In fact, sometimes they look worse than us. Sometimes we get a little boost of self-satisfaction when we see we're doing better than them in the hair/weight/looks department. Aspirational is out and authentic is in. Aspirational is no longer working for a lot of brands. Authenticity is gaining market share.

We can thank COVID-19 for the rise of UGC. No, really. *Fast Company* did a study on this trend in 2022 and found that when the pandemic hit, big-budget, highly produced ad shoots were tabled. While we waited for life to "return to normal," brands found that UGC enjoyed better outcomes with consumers because of its authenticity and attainability. For many, there was no reason to go back to paying millions for celebrity endorsements or top dollar to influencers.

This authentic approach dovetails nicely with a rising trend in consumer behavior: increasing numbers of people check a product's reviews before they even look at its details or price. We're relying more and more on the authentic opinions of people like us to help us make informed buying decisions. We can smell when we're being "sold" to but find all-natural word of mouth to be the source of truth.

Another way brands gain authenticity (and market share) is by having a genuine, personable voice. Who among us hasn't accidentally spent too much time scrolling through Twitter "wars" between fast-food chains or followed a brand for no other reason than their funny and relatable posts? (I'm looking at you, Oklahoma Department of Wildlife.) Consumers also react positively when a brand appears to stand up for a value that they share. Think: Coca-Cola's social impact push or Dove's "campaign for real beauty."

Implausibly enough, we can translate what works for brands so that it serves us. Owning who we are, not trying to be overly sales-y, and remembering the value of good reviews, these things are key to being a Unicorn.

### WHO IS AUTHENTIC? GRETA THUNBERG

Whether it's Asperger's, teenage contrarianism, her passion for the planet, or a combination of all three, Greta Thunberg calls it like she sees it. And what you see with Thunberg is what you get. She is vocal in her denouncement of people and practices that harm the environment. She blasts aviation as dire for the atmosphere's carbon load, so she famously travels in more environmentally responsible ways, a stunt that works double duty: she's practicing what she preaches while exposing how inaccessible environmentally conscious travel is for everyday people. There will never be an exposé of Greta Thunberg. We will never see another side of her because there is no other side of her. Paparazzi can wait forever, but they'll never get a snap of Greta Thunberg on a private jet, eating whale, or burning a pile of tires in her yard. Whatever your opinion of her, climate activist Greta Thunberg is undeniably authentic.

## WHAT WE'VE SEEN

I was playing golf recently with a person I believe is one of the Authentic. I asked about his career, and he told me of a strong and rapid rise through his time at Uber. I asked why he left. His answer, "I got fired." That was refreshingly authentic.

### *Authenticity isn't perfection*

The keys for authenticity are not the same as the keys for perfection. In fact, perfection can be a real turnoff.

Have you ever been fired? I have. Have you ever admitted it? In my interviews over the years, I ask this question. How many people actually said in their interviews that they got fired from a job? In my experience, the answer is something like 0.5 percent.

For those who do admit it, I get all sorts of variations on why. "We had philosophical differences." "The company merged with another one and there were redundancies." Or my favorite: "I felt like my season had come to a close there." Maybe I'm becoming jaded, but when I hear that a "season has come to a close," I really want to follow up by asking if it was a misdemeanor or a felony.

After interviewing thousands of candidates, I foresee a different future from our present, where we bury our mistakes and gloss over our struggles. I believe we are well on our way to seeing the authentic get rewarded and elevated from the crowd of pretenders.

### WHY HIRING MANAGERS LOVE THE AUTHENTIC

Finding out the person you've hired isn't what they seem is every hiring manager's nightmare. Be bad at your job, be late, skip your onboarding paperwork: they can deal with these issues. Just don't be inauthentic. Inauthentic leads to squandered resources, lawsuits, and PR nightmares.

Tips for cultivating authenticity at work:

- Model it.
- Make your space psychologically safe, ensuring staff know they can be themselves without repercussions (as long as

they're respectful and "being tr

any other HR policies).

- Incorporate authenticity into company v*olate*

*Authenticity is about telling the truth and not always in the most winsome light*

But how much truth? My dad was a small-town lawyer in North Carolina (think Mayberry) preparing a man named Amos for being a witness in an automobile accident case. Amos was a gas station attendant who worked in the busiest part of town—the intersection of our two main roads. That meant it had four lanes and not just a flashing light.

Dad prepared Amos for the next day's trial. Amos was the star witness (as he was in most auto cases in my hometown). But Dad struggled at first. He couldn't get him to say anything when asking him practice questions. Amos just kept saying, "I don't recall."

It was all he said, over and over. Dad told him he needed to open up. Then Amos spent forever talking, telling every detail. Dad stopped him again and tried to explain how being a good witness means telling what you know, but in the right amounts. Amos says to my dad, "Mr. Vanderbloemen, let me see if I understand. Are you saying, 'Always tell the truth, just don't always be a tellin' it?'"

Dad said that is—in one sentence—at least half of what he learned in law school.

*ilures*

Be mentor told me a long time ago, "People will nod at ses. They will laugh with you at your slipups. But they ember you for how you handled the failures."

remember, early in my days of executive search, interviewing young pastor, let's call him John, for a job at a new church. He couldn't have been older than twenty-five, and we had a great time interviewing. He was candid and open, and much less nervous than I would have expected him to be. Heck, he was more poised and self-assured than candidates twice his age with twice his qualifications.

(Sidenote: When offered water or coffee, he accepted coffee, even saying what his preference was. Most candidates politely decline. He wasn't afraid to be his authentic self. I suggest you do the same next time you're offered a beverage. Just don't make yours a brandy old-fashioned if you're in a professional setting, unless that professional setting is in Wisconsin and it's after four thirty.)

John made jokes and was able to give as good as he got in the banter department. Then as now, at the end of every interview I would ask something to try to determine whether there were any skeletons in the closet or surprises that the future employer should know about. And as a young guy, I used to fumble all over that question. I remember asking him, "Do you have any moral failures in your past?"

The young candidate looked at me and said, "Mr. Vanderbloemen, I am a moral failure."

His answer shocked me. But he got the job. (Don't get me wrong; John's "moral failure" answer was from his theological perspective, in the "we've all sinned and fallen short of the glory of God" sense of moral failure. As far as the broader brushstrokes of the Ten

Commandments and the laws of the United States went, he was in the clear.)

Now, John is a fantastic guy, with some of the most integrity I've ever seen. He's always tried to do what is right and has given his life to creating more good in the world. But, oh boy, after he told me he was a moral failure, he went on to give the most authentic answer I'd ever heard.

John entered college about the same time the internet became mainstream. And when the internet became mainstream, so did inappropriate content on the internet. I can't imagine how many people would've gotten in trouble for looking at inappropriate sites if they'd been available to all the generations before John's.

When John was early in college, he stumbled across some websites he shouldn't have been looking at. After a period of time, he realized he really needed to tell his girlfriend (who is now his wife) about this issue. He also sought counseling. He told me all of this, and I responded by saying, "Well, what did you do about it?"

"I sought counseling."

"Okay, what kind of counseling?"

"I found a guy who used to be a Marine drill sergeant," John said. "You had to apply to become one of the people he would counsel. I got in and went to my first meeting. He told me that we would have to meet with my girlfriend and that he was going to hook me up to a polygraph and then ask me about my entire sexual history. With my girlfriend present."

John's honesty floored me. At the same time I made a mental note to never hire a former Marine to be your counselor.

John kept going to counseling for a long time. In fact, the counselor finally told John that he'd recovered, and he needed to quit coming to counseling.

John showed an amazing ability to learn from his mistakes. He even used his story as part of his own journey, as he talked to a young man who worked for him. It became a powerful lesson to me about how those who are brave enough to be authentic, those who truly stand out, are able to take their failures and turn them into pivots toward success.

Everyone's made mistakes. Authentic people can share those mistakes appropriately.

## Report from the Unicorns

Of our survey respondents, 17.36 percent —the most for any trait— report that they're strongest in authenticity. Being authentic is good for your professional life, like so many Unicorn traits. And, again, like so many Unicorn traits, it's good for your personal life as well.

## Building better relationships

Being authentic builds confidence and trust among your team, two types of relational equity worth their weight in gold, according to our Unicorns.

Andy P. says, "I believe authenticity may be one of the most important attributes in team building. Authenticity breeds confidence. Authenticity also breeds trust because it helps your team believe you are who you say you are. I recently had a teammate who was struggling to meet her metrics. I needed to call this to her attention, but in the same breath I admitted my own mistake in not staying on top of our metrics. In doing so, I called her to the standard but remained authentic in letting her know I had fallen short too. The result of our interaction was deeper trust and confidence in the leadership I was providing."

"People hunger for authenticity from their leaders," says Angela F. "Being vulnerable and open about our strengths and weaknesses helps build bridges and trust. We could all use a bit more of that."

Relating to people in a more intentional way is another by-product of being authentic, says Monique T.: "I strongly believe that you gain more true respect from others when you are your authentic self. When we are authentic we help break down walls that keep us from being approachable. I think being authentic also helps in other areas, especially in being connected to others in developing true meaningful relationships. This helps people feel safe to be their authentic selves too."

As someone who does a lot of public speaking, Glenn S. says being transparent helps connect with an audience: "It opens the door to real relationships. Being vulnerable is the beginning of others admitting their failures and helps them to drop their mask of perfection."

## Like finds like, and safe learns safe

Thomas S. shares a more nuanced benefit of being authentic. He says, "Authenticity provides two primary benefits: it draws or attracts like-minded people, and it drives away people who are not like minded."

Authenticity also leads to psychological safety. When you're authentic, people know how you are and what they're getting. We've all had bosses who were unpredictable to the point that you never knew when they would be giving the office a half day after a pizza party at lunch or when they'd pop in at five thirty on a Friday demanding that report that's due in two weeks. When we don't know a person's true self, it makes us feel anxious and unsafe.

Leigh Anne B. says, "I have learned in my position the importance of being the same person in all circumstances. It helps when the people on my team know who I am and also know that I am consistent in the decision-making process. That means many times they know how I am going to react or respond to situations, and that builds a better working team. It takes the unknown out of the equation and gives more stability to a working relationship."

"I live fully myself in every area of my life—home, work, the gym, church, etc.," says Holly J. "It is vital for people to see and trust my authentic self. It helps people feel safe, seen, and able to be themselves."

Sally M. has also seen the benefits of being herself 24-7 and how it opens the door for others to be authentic as well. "I am definitely a 'what you see is what you get' kind of person. I feel that being open and honest with people, even if that makes me vulnerable, puts people at ease and comfortable to be their authentic selves. It does not guarantee people will be authentic with you, but I believe it helps."

## It's less work

Consider the following fictional characters: Michael Dorsey, bachelors Kip and Henry, Daniel Hillard, exiled Chicagoans Joe and Jerry, and Viola Johnson. (Better known as *Tootsie*, Tom Hanks's and Peter Scolari's characters in *Bosom Buddies*, *Mrs. Doubtfire*, Tony Curtis's and Jack Lemmon's characters in *Some Like It Hot*, and Amanda Bynes's character in *She's the Man*.) What do they all have in common? Each spent a ton of time and energy hiding their authentic selves. Were their journeys thought-provoking, heartwarming, and at times hilarious? Sure. But the only moral I've ever drawn from their stories is: it's a lot less work to just be yourself, and besides, you always get caught.

You won't see Brendan P. going to absurd lengths to hide his true self: "People pick up on a lack of consistency very quickly, and it is far easier to lose credibility than it is to build it," he cautions. "In the same way simply telling the truth keeps one from having to keep track of multiple versions of lies; staying intentionally consistent and authentic frees someone from having to keep track of how they appear or present themselves in different contexts. It is far easier to manage, it preserves reputation, and presents opportunities to engage with people."

Kristen M. agrees: "It is truly best to own who you are. People often forgive you and offer grace when you are authentic. It also takes a *lot* more work and energy to switch back and forth."

And finally, experience has taught Frank A. that being his authentic self is the only way to be. He says, "As a twice-wounded combat veteran, I realize that life is short and fragile. I am not duplicitous, and I am the same person 24-7-365."

## WHAT WE DO

No matter what the content of your character, it's much more difficult to live an inauthentic life. *Inventing Anna* is not just another hit from Shondaland; it's a cautionary tale. Being yourself is better, if less glamorous, than convincing New York's socialite set that you're a German heiress. And it will help you stay out of jail.

### Transparency at Vanderbloemen

You won't be surprised to hear how much we value transparency at Vanderbloemen. If something I have to discuss with a colleague isn't confidential, I have a habit of always leaving doors open, having conversations in a hallway or common space, and not being cagey about who can hear me. I like knowing that my team can overhear anything I'm saying. It builds confidence and trust.

So does honesty, as I've mentioned. When I'm doing an interview and someone isn't afraid to admit when they've gotten fired, those candidates always get a bump in credit.

It's refreshing when someone is so forthright. I remember when Anna (different Anna, not Anna Delvey) told me about her career and what had gone well. She was very accomplished, had risen through the career ranks, but had one stutter step on a résumé. When I asked her about it, she simply said, "I got fired. I got fired because I made bad decisions and didn't follow through on my work. And if I were my manager back then, I would've fired me too."

That seems like something that would cost Anna the interview with me, but it actually went exactly the opposite way. Why? Because in these high stakes situations, people aren't typically transparent. People aren't usually authentic. If you can spot someone who is authentic, you've spotted someone who stands out of the crowd. If you want to be a Unicorn, I'd suggest you get comfortable with authenticity.

*Here's How*

Don't be afraid to share examples of where you've messed up, as John did when I was interviewing him. But there's no reason to overdo it. Share, but don't overshare. Authentic people have a way of sharing their mistakes with humility, bringing people together. Learn from them and you'll learn to be authentic.

ADMIT YOUR MISTAKES

This doesn't mean putting yourself up on a cross or hiring a tall nun to walk next to you crying, "Shame" all the time. Admit your mistakes, admit you're struggling, and move on.

For Diana A., it was liberating to come to this conclusion. "I have always been authentic but not always willing to own up to my mistakes. Finally, I was in a position where I had to own my mistakes. Once I did, I learned how freeing that is. To be able to acknowledge one's failing is to be able to grow faster and healthier. 'The truth shall set you free' is completely true."

Not only are these practices good for cultivating authenticity, it turns out making mistakes and owning them helps us learn and retain knowledge much better than if we'd gotten it "right" in the first place. In studies, researchers have discovered the importance of admitting mistakes and receiving "corrective feedback, including analysis of the reasoning leading up to the mistake," concluding that mistakes made and corrected when the stakes are low lead to far fewer mistakes when the stakes are high. So go ahead: admit your mistakes and learn from them now so you get it right the next time.

## ADMIT WHEN YOU'RE STRUGGLING

Humility again plays a role here. Admitting you don't have it all figured out is both authentic and helpful for finding solutions to what challenges you.

"When I am struggling, I do not hide it," says Glenn H. "I find my openness, and not trying to be someone I am not, helps others to be receptive to what I have to say."

This isn't easy, says Chad S., especially if you're used to being in a position of authority. "Leaders are often reluctant to share their struggles or when they don't know the answers. But when the people you're leading see that level of authenticity, they often extend an extra measure of grace and patience. Being authentic doesn't mean it's easy. It just means fewer roadblocks on the way to solutions."

## SPEND YOUR AUTHENTICITY WISELY

Remember that you can't please everyone, no matter how authentic you are.

"Adopting the mindset that pleasing everyone is not possible will set you free," says Sam T. "If you are spending your valuable mental and emotional energy worrying about whether or not you are pleasing everyone, you are wasting that energy."

### AUTHENTICITY RED FLAGS

There's authentic and then there's theatrics. Vulnerability can build bridges, but when it's not 100 percent authentic, it becomes manipulative. Ask yourself these questions to avoid veering into the histrionic:

- Am I leading with my pain for genuine reasons or because vulnerability is trendy, and I know this could be a shortcut?

- Is my "authenticity" making me a martyr? Very few people can actually own their problem. A counselor once told me, "Everyone gets through divorces. But the people that actually heal from them are the people who can name what part of the failed marriage was their fault. Very few people do this, but the few that do recover quicker."

- Is what I'm putting out into the world helpful? Being authentic doesn't mean airing your grievances left and right. And it doesn't give you the right to be a jerk. Think before you speak.

## AUTHENTIC TAKEAWAYS

- Our brains crave authentic.
- Authenticity can do a lot of the heavy lifting for you in terms of building trust and confidence.
- You don't have to be perfect, just authentic.
- Mistakes are okay and make you better.
- Being authentic is easier than keeping an untouched frosted cake in the fridge in case you need to stick your face in it when your estranged wife comes over unexpectedly.

# THREE

# THE AGILE

With a toddler at home, a parent can't help but become agile. If anything can keep a person on their toes, it's a tiny human with insatiable curiosity, questionable judgment, and the mobility to pick up small, expensive objects and fling them into the nearest toilet.

I'd always considered myself pretty spry for a toddler dad until I was stretching in the living room and Macy came to "help." She started doing her version of stretching. It was like she suddenly became a master of Ashtanga yoga. She was the cutest pretzel anyone has ever seen.

Meanwhile, I was struggling to touch my toes.

It dawned on me: every day I am alive, I get less flexible. And it's not just me. It's all of us.

**Agile fact:** A physical therapist friend told me the other day about a continuing education class she'd taken over the weekend. It was on geriatric physical therapy, and she shared a sobering fact: once a person is no longer able to get up off the floor on their own, their life expectancy is less than five years. Practice agility, friends!

### WHO IS AGILE? LIZZO

She wasn't born here, but we Houstonians are proud to claim Lizzo as one of our own. Lizzo is a classically trained flutist who incorporates that talent into her performances, all while doing choreography that would put most people's cardio routines to shame. Being one of the most physically agile performers around today is just part of Lizzo's agile reputation. In 2022, she released a song called "Grrrls," which contained a word that is considered an ableist slur. When her Instagram followers told her this, Lizzo immediately rewrote the lyric telling her fans, "As a fat black woman in America, I've had many hurtful words used against me so I overstand the power words can have (whether intentionally or in my case, unintentionally)." This was a move of pure agility: the agility to respond and change quickly as well as the agility to learn and grow as a person.

## WHAT WE KNOW

We don't need science to tell us what we see happening in real time: the older we get, the harder it is to play ninety minutes of soccer or remember why you walked into the kitchen. A study in *Scientific American* on learning a new language concluded that fluency is much more difficult to achieve as an adult. Young learners, however, seem to pick up Mandarin as easily as they can pick up their clothes from the floor. (Of course, every parent knows that just because the kids *can* doesn't mean they *will*.) Children's minds are as bendy as their bodies. Until they're not.

Getting older means getting less agile. Every day, we lose a little bit of that flexibility, a tiny path in our plastic minds.

Something similar happens to teams and organizations. Think about how you operate at work: Are your meeting structures and operations functions of "because that's how we've always done it"? Chances are, someone long ago decided how things should be, and it's been that way ever since. In that way, we're like the cows on their path coming back into the barn for the night. Is that particular path the best one? Is it the most efficient? Who knows? It's the path they've always used. Depending on the organization's culture, questioning why things are the way they are might be detrimental to the person (to say nothing of the cow) asking. Rocking the boat is threatening to insecure leaders, and squeaky wheels sometimes get replaced completely. We hope you're not in that kind of workplace, but if you are, this is your sign to be on your way. There are better opportunities out there.

### Do you have what it takes to survive the riptide?

The world is changing, and agility is more important than ever. Canadian prime minister Justin Trudeau said, "Change is moving faster than ever, but will never move this slowly again." The world is sending us an invitation to change. If we think we can keep our heads down and wait for that invitation to go away, we're wrong. Change is a rip current and trying to swim against it is futile. The Agile know not to fight it but to swim parallel and accept change for what it is.

### The Agile are thriving

No matter what the circumstances, the Agile succeed. The pandemic showed us just how important it is for businesses to be agile. "Pivoting" and innovating were the difference between thriving and folding when COVID-19 suddenly changed the way we lived. Agile businesses are the product of agile people who—and this is important—are allowed to exercise their agility in the workplace.

It's estimated that one-third of small businesses did not survive the pandemic. There are many reasons why this happened: small businesses simply didn't have the resources to weather the storm, big box stores were better able to adapt, or suddenly theirs was a product no one could use anymore. At Vanderbloemen, we were just as concerned about how the pandemic would hurt us as any other small business. You'll recall that there wasn't a lot of in-person worshipping going on, so suddenly searching for a new church leader wasn't as hot an item for many churches. Additionally, churches were themselves suffering from the consequences of the pandemic.

I remember thinking, "Well, if we're going to go down, we can at least go down swinging." We started a new service offering: Vanderbloemen Teams. It was a scaled-back version of our services that helped place the right people in the right places, but it wasn't as costly as the complete package that is our gold search standard. Agility got us through, and I'm pleased to say the business is doing better than ever. But it wasn't just us. Many of our clients and colleagues were able to stay agile and find new ways of thriving during the pandemic.

### Diversity is good for agility

Diversity is a huge accelerant of agility. Diverse thoughts, diverse voices, ages, backgrounds, and cultures make stronger teams. With the workforce becoming more diverse and incorporating much-needed DEI (diversity, equity, and inclusion) initiatives, those who are agile will rise to the top. At this moment, according to the Business Agility Institute, diversity is not valued as a core component of agility. I can tell you right now that this is going to change. We can't be agile—as people or organizations—if we don't embrace diversity.

## WHY HIRING MANAGERS SEEK THE AGILE

The Agile are generally positive people who can problem-solve. They'll roll with changes, adapt quickly, and push back only when absolutely necessary: a hiring manager's dream.

**Tips for cultivating agility at work:**
Agility advocates Clement B. and Ryan B. give us their best advice for this.

- Don't add waste to projects; simplify things.
- Don't waste time during meetings.
- Don't have meetings at all if you can help it.
- Okay, if you must have meetings, make them short and focused.
- Consider risk management at all points to reduce the possibility of problems in the future.
- Always look for ways to tweak the status quo and modify processes to work for your own team's needs.
- Don't be afraid of upsetting others with change.
- Celebrate being agile and celebrate when being agile moves the ball.

## WHAT WE'VE SEEN

*Agility tests*

When I am interviewing a candidate and want to find out how agile they might be, I ask these three questions:

1. What new skill are you learning?
2. What new hobby have you developed?
3. What part of history do you like studying the most?
   (Sometimes agility is the ability to look backward.)

Another thing I've been known to do to test agility in a potential candidate even before the interview starts is change the interview location. I know this sounds a little cagey, but I assure you it's not as bad as it sounds. I always give at least two hours' notice, and I never move the location very far from the original spot in case transportation is an issue. It's always across the street or around the corner. How candidates handle this is always a great indicator of how well they will fit in with our culture at Vanderbloemen.

*Report from the Unicorns*

Among our survey of Unicorns, 5.87 percent of respondents identified agility as their dominant trait.

Russ B. tells us how agility helps him solve old problems with new ideas. "I find more and more things are being done 'because that's the way they've always been done.' Too often organizations fall into complacency, finding a solution that worked once and sticking to it stubbornly. Similarly, I find that when I address problems, they are deemed unsolvable—too expensive or can't be done—and I'm sure that was the case a decade or two ago when the problem arose. What I'm finding is that these problems then need to be read-dressed every so often since technologies and solutions are always changing and evolving."

He gives an example of this. He was told there's no way to get a wireless remote for advancing presentation slides. The space was simply too big, he was told. Any remote that reached that far would cost a fortune. "Okay, but that information was from ten years ago," he tells us. "I took thirty minutes to revisit the problem. Thanks to the growth in Bluetooth technology, I found a little twenty-dollar remote that perfectly does the trick. We need to be agile, not just to pivot quickly but to look at old problems through new lenses."

## WHAT WE DO

A CCO candidate I was interviewing and her daughter were counting down the days to their bucket-list trip to France when the pandemic hit. Suddenly, instead of nibbling *pain au chocolat* by the Seine, they were faced with months of the same old, same old at home. Naturally, they were quite disappointed. Once they had mourned the fact that their trip would have to come later, my CCO focused on what she could do in the meantime. She could learn French. She committed to learning French in preparation for the trip that would, eventually, happen.

Sometimes being agile simply means making *tarte au citron* when life hands you lemons.

### Accept it and move on

Have you ever heard the phrase "build a bridge and get over it"? That's what agile people do when something changes. Jonathan H.

says this is an important part of becoming agile. "The quicker you realize the fact of the new reality, the more quickly you can move forward in it," he says.

Kalena H. agrees: "Understanding that things change in an organization helps me be a better team player. I don't get frustrated when a procedure or policy changes. I'm flexible and roll with it."

For Derek F., learning to be agile in the face of change has made him a better leader. "For me, the biggest thing that helped me become more agile is simply understanding that change is unavoidable. No matter what you do in your life, you will encounter change. You can either get frustrated or grow with it. Once I realized this, change became much easier for me to deal with. In fact, it pushed me toward being who I am today, a person who not only embraces change but looks for opportunities to create changes that can make things better."

### Stay humble

You're going to hear this a lot as we examine the twelve traits. Humility plays a role in nearly all of them. When you're able to set aside your ego, your ability to become a Unicorn increases exponentially.

Nick D. says, "It's helpful to not be attached to your own ideas. Be open to new thoughts and new ways of doing things. Always assume there's a better way to do something than what you are currently doing. Never stop learning and growing."

"One way that I've become more agile is to learn to not take outcomes personally," adds Chris H. "If things change, or details I've worked on need to be replaced or scrapped, it's a quick and creative part of the process."

"Practice humility to ensure you aren't tied to your pathway," recommends Dave H. "If things need to change, making sure your idea isn't tied to your value helps you to be much more agile."

## Make it science

Kyle T. recommends taking a scientific approach. It's easier to be agile when you're looking at a situation with data and metrics in mind rather than feelings: "View things as an experiment. If they work, keep doing them. If they don't, what adjustments need to be made? If adjustments don't work, try a completely different idea that might accomplish the purpose or goal."

## Remember the mission

Another good way to practice your agility is to keep your mission front and center. Anyone who's ever run a company or started one knows the importance of mission. Your mission is your North Star and should drive every single decision you make. This makes it easier to be agile in the face of challenges. If it supports the mission, it's a yes. If not, move on. Spoiler alert: this will come up again when we talk about being purpose driven.

Erika M. says, "Being agile comes back to believing the mission of your organization is bigger than what you have in front of you. When we do that, we can put aside our preferences and change when we are asked. It's about being able to think beyond your position, beyond yourself."

Fox Z. agrees on the importance of a bigger picture. "Too many people crack and quit because things change. Do not be intimidated by those types of environments. Be willing to stick with the changes, try new things even if you fail, and keep a healthy perspective on the big picture over the small one."

## AGILE TAKEAWAYS

- We're becoming less agile every day.
- Our brains need to be stretched as much as our bodies.
- Doing things because "that's the way we've always done them" is toxic in the workplace.
- Agility thrives on diversity, new ideas, and fresh experiences.

# FOUR

# THE SOLVER

## CASE STUDY: THE SOLVER UNICORN

Kevin Plank sweats. A lot. He was also a college football player in the late '90s, a time when cotton was king for athletic clothing. And it was king only because a better fabric didn't exist. Frustrated by this, Plank decided to solve the problem. Scraping together all the money he could, Plank started researching synthetic fabrics that could do a better job keeping athletes comfortable as they sweat. His first year in business, he made $17,000 in sales. While the start was promising, it wasn't where Plank wanted to be. To solve the slow sales problem, which he believed was a result of being an unknown in the market, Plank took nearly everything he (and the company) had and bought a full page ad in *ESPN The Magazine* for $25,000. The gamble paid off and the next year Plank's company, Under Armour, hit more than $1 million in sales. And the rest, as they say, is history, all thanks to a Solver.

When faced with challenges, people can either choose to be on the problem side of the equation or the solution side. Those who choose to find solutions, who refuse to be victims, and who spend energy moving past those challenges are irreplaceable. The ability to keep your head in a panicked, rushed situation will set you apart from the crowd. I've discovered a particular mindset that is prevalent in the Solvers I've met and interviewed over the years. This chapter will give you a path to become an exceptional Solver that cannot go unnoticed. And in a world that is moving faster and proving less certain than ever, developing this ability will raise your value like never before.

Early in my career, I ran across a great older man who became a mentor to me. Jack Hart was an executive for Palm Pilot (if you can remember that far back) and was head of all their HR and people solutions. The company was a very early tech company. It grew really fast, and it got really messy. As someone once told me, you can have control or you can have growth, but you can't have both. So Jack's job was detangling the chaos that came with growth.

Jack was also on the board of the church that I had inherited. Before I got there, the church had been through two splits in the last six years. These were not splits over small disagreements. These were big debates, all emotionally charged. The kind of emotional charge that can supersede rationale and friendship, and cause life-long friends to scream at each other.

There were very few people that everyone seemed to think were on the solution side of every argument. Lots of friendships got ruined. Family relationships got tense. And a whole lot of people were pointing fingers at one another. But Jack had a knack for having everyone like him. Everyone on every side of every issue liked Jack.

I asked him about this one time, and he said to me: "William, everyone falls into one of two categories. People are either on the problem side of the equation, or they are on the solution side. When I lay down to die, I'd love for people to stand up and say Jack was always on the solution side."

I buried Jack later that year and told that story. Then people from all three churches that were the result of the church splits got up in sequence to speak. I don't think I've ever seen that much conflict resolved at one funeral. People from all three sides said yes, Jack was part of the solution and never part of the problem.

## WHAT WE KNOW

In our research we found that the top 1 percent of all people we've interviewed showed an uncanny knack to look at the solution side of an issue and not the problem side of an issue. I probably saw this best during the pandemic and interviews we did during that time. Trying to do our normal search process all on Zoom became a new complexity and a new opportunity. And it was amazing to see the hiring organizations, which ranged from very old traditional businesses to high-tech companies, balk at the new world order. No matter what the industry, most people fell back on something along the lines of "we've never done it that way before; we can't do it now" (remember the cows from chapter 3, "The Agile"?). But a small percentage of people and companies rose to the challenge and said, "Here's a solution. What if we did it this way?"

### Complaining is fun!

Our brains are negative biased. Think about it: When our ancestors peeped out of the cave, was it in their best interests to see and admire the good things, like that lovely copse of May apples blooming over there? Or would it have served them better to clock the wild hyenas, foul-smelling water source, and extinguished fire? Which ones are you going to tell the group about? Gratitude makes our lives better, but for early people, recognizing and voicing the negative made their lives last.

Plus, complaining gives us a lot of positive reinforcement. It makes us think we're smarter than the powers that be, and it helps us bond with a group. Ask anyone who is friends with their very first coworkers from decades ago. Did breakfast sandwiches in the cafeteria and half-day summer Fridays bind them? Or was it a common enemy and a mutual sense of injustice that they could vent to one another about?

But complaining isn't all it's cracked up to be. It has a negative impact on your brain and, not surprisingly, a negative impact on your company culture. It's better to be a Solver.

There's a reason Dale Carnegie's first rule of winning friends and influencing people is "Don't criticize, condemn, or complain." While complaining can score points in your immediate sphere of influence, it's never going to help you rise above. To rise above, you need to be a Solver.

## Okay, I'll be a Solver, but I'll do it on my own, thanks

Remember the old joke "What is a camel? A horse drawn by committee." Even though there is a higher risk of error, solving is better when done with a group. If you're like my kids, however, you might hate this kind of group project. In school, you might have always been the one doing the heavy lifting in the group project department. Chances are, if you're reading this book, you were. My kids hated group projects for a variety of reasons. It was like being in the Tour de France, stuck in the peloton doing the work while some other kids just hung out behind you, drafting and thinking of how they were going to style their yellow jersey. It seems like my kids always ended up doing all the work. Group projects were cumbersome and slow moving. They had less control when they had to collaborate. The old leadership aphorism got a twist in our household: if you want to go fast and far, go alone.

Solving problems in a group can be threatening, exhausting, and frustrating, but studies show that, when they're done right, group projects in a professional setting lead to innovation that wouldn't otherwise have happened.

## The millennials on board

You know who does like to solve things in a group setting? Millennials. Congratulations if you're a member of this generation. You're more likely to be better at adjusting to whatever the workforce throws your way. You're also better at dealing with conflict. These qualities correlate with successful workplace collaborations. Not surprisingly, millennials value collaboration and are some of the most successful Solvers.

## There's no "I" in Solvers

When I was just starting out, very little positive criticism made it through to my brain, and when it did, I'm sorry to say it wasn't received positively. I was young and certain I knew everything.

There was one exception, however. I remember giving a presentation about our vision for the next year and all of the things we were going to get done as an organization. An older person, who would become my mentor, was in the audience. I asked him, "Jack, what did you think of the presentation?"

He said, "William, I had no idea you were going to get so much done in the next year!" I explained to him that this was what the *organization* would get done and that it was going to be amazing.

Then Jack looked at me and said, "Then why did you keep saying the word *I* instead of the word *we?*"

Never use *I* when you could use *we*.

## WHY HIRING MANAGERS LOVE THE SOLVERS

When's the last time you went to HR with something good? Enough said.

**Tips for cultivating a Solver mentality at work:**

- Encourage humility and lifelong learning.
- Celebrate Solver victories and give credit to individuals where it's due.
- Ask that staff bring solutions to the table at each meeting; even if they're bombastic and unachievable, it puts them in the right mindset.
- Language counts: rebrand "problems" as "possibilities."

## WHO IS A SOLVER? JENNIFER GARNER

Jennifer Garner is a terrific actress and seemingly universally beloved. She's also a Solver. Perhaps it's from playing one on TV in her breakout role on *Alias*, or perhaps it's because she believes strongly in the inherent goodness of people. Maybe a combination thereof. Regardless, we've seen Jennifer Garner in the spotlight for decades now, and it's as a Solver every time. Garner shares three children with her ex-husband Ben Affleck, and no matter what was reported on in the tabloids or how difficult it must have been, Garner has always projected a cheery, collaborative image. She says she respects Affleck's old flame and new wife, Jennifer Lopez, as a fellow mother and has nothing but kind words for the couple and their co-parenting relationship.

Garner seems particularly interested in solving problems for children, her own and others. As an activist, she's worked to pass legislation to protect celebrities' children from paparazzi. She's also an ambassador for Save the Children US, supporting children's literacy, education, and nutrition. Frustrated with the lack of healthy baby food options, she started an organic baby food line. To make sure it was available to all children, she saw to it that it became the first of its kind available to families receiving food stamps.

## WHAT WE'VE SEEN

A solving mentality has helped Vanderbloemen succeed. The business is, of course, here to solve problems, so solutions are built into our company framework. But even for people who don't run an executive search firm, being a Solver will help you go far. A solving mentality is what got me here in the first place. I saw that executive search was leaving out a considerable market, so I built Vanderbloemen to solve that problem.

In our interviews, we have gotten pretty keen at listening to how often a candidate says "we" versus "I." It's become an unspoken litmus test for us. Why? Because we have become convinced that most people are selfish (sometimes for good reasons) and that the people who lead with "we" are both exceptional and amazingly valuable in whatever situation you find them.

## Report from the Unicorns

Our Unicorns have lots of reasons being a Solver helps in work and life. Whether it's the feel-good feeling that comes with a problem solved, the lessons you learn, or the positives of having a Solver mindset, there are plenty of reasons to be a Solver.

## Solving makes you feel good!

"Bringing solutions is extremely gratifying," says Steve B. "Seeing others benefit from concepts and strategies I have found and developed brings joy to my work and life."

"You could complain or be a Solver," says JoAnn F. "And I think it is more fun and productive to find a way to solve a problem than to complain about it."

"One of the strongest qualities I have is being a Solver," says Hanna S. "Complaining and stressing never help a situation. They are natural human responses to chaos and conflict but are not helpful. I try to focus on the next step or the solution to get things done. When you think about solving the problem versus the problem itself, you are more likely to stress less and get to a solution quicker. On top of that, you can move forward and feel accomplished and ready for the next thing."

### Solving helps you learn and avoid repeating the problem

Meagan M. says, "As a Solver, I have the keen ability to look at an issue, accept whatever happened in the past that has led us to where we are in the present, and create a solution so the situation does not repeat itself in the future. It is imperative to remain calm when you are a Solver."

### Solving is a winning mindset

Donna B. says, "It has always been essential in leadership to have potential solutions ready to bring to the table. I do not have to solve all of the issues and certainly desire input, but as the leader I need to have thought it through and be ready to offer effective solutions. I improve by playing out scenarios and using my faith, research, wisdom, and other best practices to discern solutions. I am always thinking 'how can we do better?' With this mindset, I can be on the solution side of the equation in most situations."

**Solver fact:** It was the late-twentieth-century scribe Robert Matthew Van Winkel who famously self-identified as a Solver in a ditty containing the line "If there was a problem, yo, I'll solve it / Check out the hook while my DJ revolves it."

(Robert performed this song as his hip-hop alter ego, Vanilla Ice.)

## WHAT WE DO

When I was starting out in leadership, I remember growing weary of people bringing me complaints. I was talking to a mentor about this, and he gave me a great solution.

He said, "William, I very rarely have people come to me with complaints anymore."

I asked how that could be.

He said, "I simply made it a rule that no one could come to me with a problem unless they also came with a solution. And that drastically reduced the number of complaints I received because not many people are good at finding solutions."

Unicorns are good at finding solutions, especially the 14.06 percent of them who identify as strongest in this area. Wondering how to become a Solver yourself? The Solvers have solutions.

### Come with a solution

It doesn't have to be *the* solution or even a good solution. But to become a Solver, you need to start somewhere. As my mentor told me all those years ago, extend the same parameters (no problem raised without a solution) and grace (the solution doesn't have to be perfect) to yourself that you'd extend to others. Business experts have recently blasted this practice as intimidating and harmful, but when you do it our way, it's not. It's true, I like to ask people to come with solutions. But they don't have to be perfect. They don't even have to be feasible. Sometimes the initial solution is, "How about we take the rest of the day off and go to the rodeo?" And while that's a solution that probably won't actually solve the problem, it's a good place to start. We're coming up with ideas, we're thinking creatively, and we have a sense of humor about it.

Asking for solutions in this way nurtures the culture. Demanding that they put a fifty-page spiral-bound proposal for what the solution should be on my desk does not.

Dustin L. says being solution focused is a mindset: "I got better at being a Solver by committing to the idea that 'If I see a problem, I need to come up with a solution.' Many people are able to point out problems and then leave them for someone else. I believe that if I see the problem, then I am capable of coming up with how to solve it. My idea may not be best, may not even be considered, but I am committed to bring something to the table."

"I am naturally analytical," says Vince L. "I decided anyone can analyze what's wrong, but not everyone can use that information to look for and be a part of the solution."

## Say yes

John A. tells us that just showing up and saying yes is the most important step to being a Solver and a Unicorn. "Get involved," he says. "Make sure you are going above and beyond in everything, especially when you're new or entry level. That earns you the opportunity to be involved in more things and ultimately gains you influence and responsibility. Simply say yes to all the opportunities to get involved that come your way."

## Look at the whole board

There's an episode of *The West Wing* in which the president is playing a game of figurative chess with another nation and literal chess with two of his staffers. As he plays, he encourages his young opponent to "see the whole board." Solvers have the ability to do just that, assessing a situation and being able to see it from all angles.

Diane B. describes how she does this: "I try to look at situations from as many viewpoints as possible prior to making a decision that will impact my team. While this can take time, I feel that it is time well spent so that I can be confident of the decision I'm making. At the same time, I value the input of others, especially those who have walked in my shoes."

"When someone on my staff brings up a problem but doesn't offer any viable solutions or possible fixes, they're not really being helpful, even though they like to see themselves as such," says Dale M. "They were like people standing on the side of the street, throwing rocks at the parade going by. I learned to always offer a possible solution or alternative when talking about something that needed to be fixed or appeared to be broken, but I never assumed it was *the* solution. One thing you learn as you move up in management roles and responsibilities is that often you don't see the complete picture."

## Break it down

"Do not be daunted by the enormity of the world's grief. Do justly now, love mercy now, walk humbly now," says the famous verse. "You are not obligated to complete the work, but neither are you free to abandon it." Solvers understand this. When big challenges come, they approach them piece by piece.

"I am a software engineer," says Susan C. "Some tasks seem insurmountable at first. I have learned over the years that taking a large problem and breaking it down into a series of smaller problems is highly beneficial. If I can solve each of the smaller problems, the big problem is solved."

"I try to narrow the questions to the most salient issues, identifying the core challenges and determining potential solutions. I try to cull out the extraneous material that doesn't move us toward a solution or that confuses the situation," says Paul S.

## Recognize if it really needs to be solved

Not everything is crying out for a solution. Be careful where you hone your Solver skills so you don't waste your time and effort. Have you ever stumbled across an item on Amazon and thought to yourself, "Does the world really *need* that?" Be prudent with your solving energy.

John D. does this by asking questions straightaway. He says, "Whenever an issue is brought up to me, I always try to find out why the person is sharing this information with me. I ask, 'Are you venting? Or are you asking me to help solve this?' Oftentimes people just need someone to listen to them. But there are those times when a solution is asked for and needed."

### SOLVER TAKEAWAYS

- Complaining, like that last cocktail of the night, is fun, but it's also bad for you.
- Never say "I" when you could say "we."
- Don't solve in a vacuum.
- Learn the difference between a problem that needs to be solved and something to let go.

## FIVE

# THE ANTICIPATOR

## CASE STUDY: THE ANTICIPATOR UNICORN

During a sabbatical that took him from India to Hawaii, the story goes, Marc Benioff had an epiphany: Why couldn't business software be as user friendly as Amazon.com? Benioff, who since his childhood had been fascinated with technology and its future, had a hunch that a business management system that "lived" completely online and required minimal up-front costs could replace the decades-old model of software that had to be installed, updated, and managed with costly hardware. He was right. Salesforce requires nothing of the user beyond internet access. Benioff and his cofounders knew Salesforce would take off and, anticipating growth, selected headquarters and office space with room to scale. As of 2022, Salesforce was one of the largest tech companies in the world and ranked 136 on the Fortune 500 list.

True confession: as a kid, I had a phase when I was taken with the idea of ESP. Maybe it was a show I had watched. Maybe it was because I read a lot of Stephen King as a nine- and ten-year-old (what were my parents thinking!?). But for whatever reason, I've always wondered if I could develop the ability to see what's coming next. To read minds and trends well enough to be able to "see around the corner."

There are some who can. They're Anticipators.

Those who anticipate rise above the crowd. They actually do almost see the future. You can too.

## WHAT WE KNOW

If your family got as attached to Netflix as mine did during the pandemic, you've likely seen *The Queen's Gambit*, a binge-worthy miniseries that beautifully illustrates the power of anticipation. Nowhere is thinking ahead more important and clearly set up than in chess. Whether you become a grandmaster or just a casual player, learning to play chess can teach you a lot about anticipating your next move and—even more important—your opponent's next move.

Our brains are the ultimate anticipators. Author Lisa Feldman Barret has done extensive research on this. She writes, "In a very real sense, predictions are just your brain having a conversation with itself. A bunch of neurons make their best guess about what will happen in the immediate future, based on whatever combination of past and present that your brain is currently conjuring."

This feature of our brains has helped us out for as long as people have been on this earth. Our hardworking brains have done everything in their power to anticipate outcomes and keep us from falling down that ravine, getting trampled by mammoths, or accidentally using our atlatls to launch a spear into our mothers-in-law. In modern times, our brains are still at it, helping us survive today's perils.

**WHO IS AN ANTICIPATOR? AARON RODGERS**

Aaron Rodgers doesn't look for the open player when he makes a pass, as any normal person would. He thinks about the desired outcome (hoisting the Lombardi Trophy high overhead while confetti showers down by way of many things, including this touchdown pass in this regular season game). Then he reads the defense and calls the play. He knows what his teammates will do. And he knows what the defense will do, maybe not five plays from now, but probably this one. He throws to an open player and makes it look easy. And it is easy. For an Anticipator.

Off the field, you have to hand it to Rodgers. He anticipates slow news days, fan reactions, and press attention. He's always ahead of the game, ready to explain it all (or be intractable) on his radio show of choice.

## You don't have to be Nostradamus

In the Old Testament, a large section of the Hebrew scriptures is given over to a section called the prophets. Prophets were able to see into the future. Prophets were valuable for helping kings out of a pickle. Prophets could anticipate.

But most scholars agree the prophets of the Old Testament were not necessarily looking five and six hundred years into the future when they were giving their prophecies. Rather, they were giving a spiritually driven commentary on how to respond to the crisis as of that minute and in the very near future. If they happened to prophesize about something five or six hundred years later: fantastic. But everyone in the moment knew that the prophet was the one who could read today's tea leaves and tell us a little bit more about tomorrow than we knew before.

You don't need to have any special psychic ability or gift. Just read the tea leaves in front of you.

### You don't need a long-term plan

I used to think that having vision as a leader meant that I could see what our ten-year plan ought to be—maybe even a twenty-year plan. The pandemic has robbed most visionary leaders of the ability to see what's next. But I'm not sure that's so bad.

We're coming out of an era of asking leaders to come up with ten- and twenty-year plans. We're moving into an era of constant change and disruption. I think this is going to give us a more accurate view of what anticipation looks like. Anticipation is when a leader can see one or two feet in front of them, one or two feet farther than the rest of the crowd. It's like that joke about the bear: you don't need to outrun the bear; you just need to outrun the guy next to you.

**Fun fact:** In the book of Psalms, David describes God's Word as a lamp unto his feet and a light unto his path. Most people think that's just a figure of speech. But what David was actually referring to were little lanterns people of the day would strap to their shoes. Those lanterns only gave them enough light to see one more step ahead—oftentimes, that's all we need.

In the pandemic, when we had to shut down quite a bit of our business, I became more focused on just trying to figure out how to respond to this week. Not this month or this year. I focused on what trends right now were affecting the next day or two. It was one of the most effective exercises in anticipation I'd done in a long time.

Now I'm looking at anticipation as something that I have to practice, focus on, and develop. Not by looking way out into the future but by seeing what's right in front of me.

## WHAT WE'VE SEEN

One of the best executive assistants I've ever met is a woman named Bethany. I had the privilege of working with her for several years, and she exhibited anticipation like very few.

Bethany didn't start as my executive assistant. She started doing office work until my assistant had to leave to be closer to family. Bethany stepped in as the interim. It's important to note that this was back in the day before iPads and smartphones, when your email wasn't at your fingertips all of the time. But we were dependent on getting back to people very quickly; that's always been a value of ours. (Remember the Fast?) One day, a lead came in right before my plane was about to take off, and it was in Spanish. So I asked Bethany, who I knew was fluent in Spanish, to read the lead and try to respond to them as best she could.

But then in the air I noticed that this wasn't Spanish; it was Portuguese. Which probably means the lead was from Brazil. Which is a place where people really don't like it when you don't know the difference between Portuguese and Spanish. I was a little bit panicked that we'd acted too soon. When I landed, I called Bethany and said just hold off on answering that lead.

She said, "Sorry, too late. I answered them. And did you know it was in Portuguese, not Spanish?"

I was pretty shocked and asked her what she had done. She replied, "Well, I found a Google translator. I used the Google translator to translate his question. Then I figured out what he was looking for and found a white paper you'd written on the subject. I ran that through Google translator, into Portuguese. And I went ahead and sent it to him. I'm so sorry I acted so fast."

Bethany went from being the interim executive assistant to executive assistant in about two minutes. She had anticipated exactly what the needs of this person were. She found technology to solve that need and had figured out the request was in Portuguese, not Spanish!

Since then, we've been on the lookout for people exactly like Bethany. We've been learning to ask questions in interviews that determine how well a person can think ahead.

## We can coach it

In our experience, anticipation is perhaps the most coachable trait of the twelve. It can be developed with a shift in mindset. I try to play golf a little bit. And I've learned by playing with the best that they all plan their tee shot based on how they want to end the hole. Good players study the pin position and wind at the green before ever deciding on a strategy for their tee shot. By the same token, the best pool players plan at least three shots ahead, just like in chess.

Candidates we interview often think only about what they need to do to get this job. Outstanding candidates are talking about how they will excel at this job so that they can fulfill their career goals. It's often thought that talking about a few jobs ahead during an interview is a mistake. It's arrogant! It's entitled! I wholeheartedly disagree.

I remember Jim, who was interviewing for a VP role at a company we represented. He asked me, "How long will the successful candidate stay in this role?" Sounds aggressive, right? Not so. The company was a very high-growth organization and stasis was not a virtue. I asked Jim why he wanted to know. He said, "Because it seems that with all of this growth, the successful candidate will be in this role for about three years before they either get promoted or hired away. If what I'm seeing is right, then I'm ready to give the best three years of my career to this role." Said the wrong way, Jim could have come off as seeing this as a stepping stone job. That would be a classic mistake. Rather, he came off as someone thinking a few shots ahead. He impressed me. He got the job. And the promotion two years later.

## Report from the Unicorns

Of our survey respondents, 8.72 percent identified as strong Anticipators. They tell me that a big part of being an Anticipator is knowing you can't anticipate everything and being able to adjust quickly.

Anticipators are cool, calm, and collected. At least that's what they appear to be. This helps in winning over everyone they engage with.

Rich G. tells us, "People often think I am cool under pressure and able to make wise, quick decisions, and that is true, but it's only because I have spent the time mentally preparing for what could happen or how people may respond. I try hard to ask myself questions that may get asked (even if they are ridiculous or would be uninformed). If I have answers for those questions, I can instill confidence in those who I am trying to influence and win over."

Jeremy H. agrees. "By spending extra time before any event preparing potential 'backup' plans, I am ready to make quick pivots while also having spent the time to think through quality contingencies ahead of time. An example of this played itself out recently over Zoom when both of my guest speakers were late for my board of directors meeting. Even though they were slotted to fill the entirety of my meeting time, I had prepared one extra discussion item for the end of the meeting. This discussion would be meaningful for my board members but was not absolutely essential if time did not permit it. Having that discussion and response time prepared beforehand allowed me to make good use of our meeting time while also buying me time to get our speakers online. It also had the added benefit of saving face for my guest speakers and was much better than if I had attempted to throw something together on the spot. The tongue-in-cheek way I often refer to this practice is, 'I'm good at being spontaneous when I've prepared to be spontaneous.'"

Mavis M. has made her ability to anticipate what people need—and the value that brings them—into a career. "Through years of experience, I've learned the value of anticipating the next event, activity, or season. I worked as a wedding coordinator for thirty-five-plus years and saw how this paid off. For more years than that, I've found great benefit in anticipating needs and recruiting people to help along the way. My supervisors all appreciate knowing that I'm already thinking about and planning for the next need."

**WHY HIRING MANAGERS LOVE ANTICIPATORS**

Anticipators naturally alleviate stress and difficult conversations for hiring managers by seeing what's coming down the road. Unicorn Tyler A. puts it best: "Anticipation helps diffuse potential conflict down the road. I was once in a very tense meeting that was hard for everyone involved. By observing the tone and tenor of the person leading the meeting, I was able to anticipate some job description changes that were coming in the next few months. By asking some open-ended questions, I was able to anticipate and identify the direction of my current position and how that might change in the future, and voiced that in a way that helped defuse the tension."

**Tips for cultivating Anticipators at work:**
- Practice solving with the end in mind.
- Encourage reading and learning history.
- Coach "thinking things through."

## WHAT WE DO

I almost did a PhD in the history of doctrine. Sounds riveting, right? It actually *is* pretty fascinating. If you want to know the future, just study the past. Humans are incredibly cyclical. (So, my wife points out, we should have seen the resurgence of "mom jeans" coming.) I see some of the culture wars that are going on right now, and they're reboots of culture wars from years gone by. That's not to minimize them; that's not to say that we shouldn't be paying attention. Rather, it just means if you study the past, you will learn the future.

### *Look behind you*

What can you do to study your past? Some of the areas that a really great Anticipator studies are:

- Family of origin. This is maybe the most common root of adult issues and behavior. Learn from your and your family's past.
- Historical patterns. Standout Anticipator Britton C. tells us, "I am a voracious reader, and I am especially drawn to history. The combination of both learning the tendencies of people, cultures, and societies and my spiritual gifting allows me to see a few steps ahead. That's my tip for anticipation: read more."

### *Practice*

Casey S. says practice makes perfect when it comes to anticipating. "My sport in high school and college was fencing. As a fencer, you have to learn to think fast and be responsive; but you also have to be able to anticipate what your opponent could do from whatever position they are in: How could they score from where they are, and how do I counter it? That training has had a direct positive impact on learning how to lead in a post-everything age. I think the key thing is to imagine possible outcomes from your circumstances as often as you can. It's the regular practice of teasing out, 'If this happens, then I will do X; but if that happens, I will do Y. And—God forbid—if the other thing happens, then we'll have no choice but to do Z.' If you do that often enough, you develop the ability to anticipate what's going to happen."

Tammy K. agrees: "Play the situation out in advance in your mind. Anticipate potential outcomes."

Sara S. says the stage helped her with this skill: "In high school and college, I did a little bit of stage managing both with my church for special events and in community theater. I really feel like that helped me prepare to learn how to be an Anticipator. There's nothing like watching an actor run onstage and then I glance at the prop table to see the prop they were supposed to take with them still sitting there."

Her biggest tip, she says, "is to stop and think through all the possibilities that could happen. Then consider how you'd need to course correct to still reach the goal. And remember, the new route to the goal may look different from what you'd anticipated. And that's okay."

*Begin with the end in mind*

We know how this works in sports, but it was Stephen Covey who put this practice on the map for business. It's probably the best piece of advice a would-be Anticipator could ever have.

Diane V. lives by this rule, saying, "I have learned that the most efficient way to keep numerous plates spinning is to envision the stated result and then list the steps necessary to get there. Deadlines are crucial, and I strive to set and meet these earlier than actually necessary. This allows me to sleep at night!"

## YOU GUESSED IT: ANTICIPATOR TAKEAWAYS

- Anticipators are next-level important.
- You don't need to see that far ahead, just farther than anyone around you.
- Learn to be a better Anticipator by knowing yourself, your history, and your surroundings.

## SIX

# THE PREPARED

## CASE STUDY: THE PREPARED UNICORN

Hardly any of us were truly prepared for COVID-19. But one leader in particular had put practices and values in place that would ensure his company's success when the world changed forever. Eric Yuan, founder and CEO of Zoom Video Conferencing (Zoom, as we know it), was more than ready for the onslaught of demand for his service. Yuan had been preparing his whole professional life for this. Having seen the successes and failures of competitors, Yuan set out to create a simple, slick way for people to communicate via video conferencing. Skype was too technology centered, with too many bells and whistles. Skype, like other competitors, tried to be more things to more people. Yuan made sure that Zoom did one thing and one thing well. He stuck to the brand's mission of developing "a people-centric cloud service that transforms the real-time collaboration experience and improves the quality and effectiveness of communications forever." By keeping the user front of mind, Yuan had prepared the perfect product. Anyone could use Zoom. Grandparents figured it out with ease. Kids had no problem adapting to it. It's user friendly to the point of foolproof. And you can use it for free. The world might not have been prepared for COVID, but Eric Yuan had prepared his product for the world.

uck happens to the prepared. Those who do their homework have always had a leg up on the field. But in today's world, learning how to prepare for a job, an interview, and a relationship has changed drastically. This chapter will give you a guidebook for preparing in the new world and a key to rising above the ordinary crowd.

John Wooden, the UCLA basketball coach who led the Bruins to ten national championships in twelve years, is beloved not only for his success on the court but the way he reached that success. You see, Coach Wooden would start every year's first practice with a lesson that would seem to fit more at a nursery school: He taught his players how to put on their socks and shoes. It wasn't that the team didn't know how to put their socks and shoes on, it was that in relearning, they remembered the details that would affect their playing. Bunched-up socks and loosely tied sneakers cause blisters, blisters affect performance, poor performance loses games, a bad record loses the chance at the championship. These small acts of preparedness, Wooden showed his team, could make all the difference.

## WHAT WE KNOW

The founder of the Scouts, Robert Baden-Powell, chose Be Prepared as the organization's motto. It means, he wrote, "You are always in a state of readiness in mind and body to do your duty; be prepared in mind by having disciplined yourself to be obedient to every order and also by having thought out beforehand any accident or situation that might occur, so that you know the right thing and the right moment, and be willing to do it."

We can take the "be obedient to every order" part out of our definition, but thinking things out beforehand is definitely the jam of Unicorns.

**Prepared fact:** Scouts founder Robert Baden-Powell wrote an eloquent final letter to the organization before his death in 1941. He urged Scouts to "try and leave this world a little better than you found it and when your turn comes to die, you can die happy in feeling that at any rate you have not wasted your time but have done your best. 'Be Prepared' in this way, to live happy and to die happy—stick to your Scout Promise always—even after you have ceased to be a boy—and God help you to do it." I'm not crying, you're crying.

### WHO IS PREPARED? ANTHONY FAUCI

From MacGyver to Mary Poppins to Russell the Junior Wilderness Explorer, we have a pretty good idea of what a prepared person is like. But what do they look like in real life? Anthony Fauci, that's who. It takes a special kind of prepared to be able to be summoned by the White House at a moment's notice and explain the finer points of immunology in language everyday people can understand. It takes an even more special kind of prepared to attempt to lead a divided nation through a pandemic with gravitas and calm. But Fauci has been preparing for this all his professional life,

having first come on the scene at the National Institute
of Health in 1968. He has been director of the National
Institute of Allergy and Infectious Diseases since 1984 and
served every president since Ronald Reagan. President
George W. Bush awarded him the Presidential Medal of
Freedom for his contributions to AIDS research. In August
2022 he announced his plans to retire from public service in
December of that year. Time will tell how well the US was
prepared for life without his guidance.

## WHAT WE'VE SEEN

One of the very best hires I ever made was my friend Holly. I had the
pleasure of working with her for more than nine years, and she came
to work alongside me very early in her career. She was twenty-three.
I interviewed her several times, but it all started with her persistence.

You see, Holly was a salesperson for a company that was trying
to win my business. And it wasn't a product I was interested in. And
I don't like sales calls. And I really don't like persistent salespeople.
But Holly just kept calling. Holly wore me out, and I finally agreed
to take a sales meeting with her. But I quickly told the two other
people working for me at the time (yes, we were that small), "One
of you all is going to have to take this meeting because I'm busy the
day that she's coming."

They asked which day she was coming. "The one when I'm
busy," I told them.

Holly came to visit the office, and a one-hour visit with my handful of a team turned into a multi-hour visit. I got back to the office later that day, and my team said: go hire her.

So we started interviewing, and in about her third interview I asked her, "So, Holly, what would you do with your first six months on the job?"

She said, "First, I need to learn our client base and what we offer. I need to learn the company. Then, I would spend the rest of my time and energy trying to convince you to do this."

She pulled out a paper with a presentation on why I should consider hiring HubSpot to run our inbound marketing. We hired HubSpot. I hired Holly. She has forever been known as Holly HubSpot. And our company has never been the same. She came to the interview prepared, intelligent, not demanding, but clear in ideas for what she would do if she were here. She exhibited so many Unicorn traits, and I've learned a lot working with her over the years.

### WHY HIRING MANAGERS LOVE THE PREPARED

When a candidate has shown that they've put in the work to learn about your company, they have an obvious advantage over candidates with a more nonchalant attitude. Playing hard to get doesn't often work with hiring managers. Best to wear your heart on your sleeve and show up more prepared than a Scout.

**How to Cultivate Preparedness at Your Work:**

- Encourage "opposition research." It's not enough to know your position on a topic; the top 1 percent know their opponents' objections and are ready to handle them.
- Practice poking holes in plans and ideas in a constructive way. This will help your team get thinking of and prepared for all scenarios.

## Report from the Unicorns

Of the Unicorns, 5.38 percent identified as Prepared. The majority spoke in the context of presentations and meetings and how important it is to have your facts straight. The benefits to being prepared are many.

## Preparation earns respect and buy-in

Steve R. tells us, "When preparing for a meeting or presentation, I am not only fully versed on the benefits of my suggested solution, I also make sure I am so familiar with any possible objections I could defend the contrary view as effectively as anyone supporting that position. I have always found knowing my position completely and being able to address any objections effectively help others see I am fully aware of all aspects of the situation." He says this helps win more arguments, as he's not seen as just "trying to push something through."

Emily V. has also experienced this and adds that being prepared is much more efficient. "Early in my career, it was pointed out by a mentor how much of the company's resources were wasted when people came to meetings late and/or unprepared. That has stuck with me over the years. I have been in various positions where I analyze processes or procedures and make recommendations as to how to improve them. Many times the person I am talking to is much more experienced than I am. If I am not prepared, and if I can't explain why my recommendations are valid and appropriate, I could easily lose the respect of the person I am trying to help."

Looking prepared is almost as important as being prepared, says Scott H.: "Being well prepared can be half the battle. If you are prepared and look and act professionally, people start out with a favorable impression of you and generally give you the benefit of the doubt. It communicates that the task, meeting, and the people involved are important and that you value their time."

## Preparation saves everyone's time

The Prepared are meeting MVPs because they often come with solutions and suggestions that obviate the need for more meetings. Says Jason M., "Taking the time to prepare for what is coming up will pay great dividends. The prep ahead of time saves significant time down the road and could be the difference between moving an organization forward and being caught in the endless spiral of meetings."

## Preparation gives you confidence

Mark E. says, "No one will ever show up to a meeting or meet with me directly and be more prepared. They may be *as* prepared but never more prepared. I have learned over the years that preparation generally solves many problems before they arise and solves existing problems more quickly and more easily. I feel as though my preparation gives me greater confidence in interactions with others, even when I ultimately don't use everything I have prepared."

## WHAT WE DO

My COO was Junior Miss Green Bay, Wisconsin, in high school. As a possessor of many Unicorn traits (she's working on Fast), she says she wasn't nervous about a lot of the competition. She had her flute solo down cold (she says even her cat could probably have played it for as much as she practiced). She had the perfect plan for her hair and makeup. Wardrobe was a cinch. The only thing that made Jennifer nervous was what she couldn't control: the interview portion. The potential questions promised to be about "the state of the world around them."

So what did she do? She studied "the state of the world" around her. Her family did too. She could tell you anything about the massacres in Rwanda or the increased fighting in Bosnia and Croatia. There wasn't a global leader she couldn't name, no endangered species she wasn't rooting for. She had the state of her world locked and loaded.

And she won the competition—even though her lowest score was on the interview.

The question ended up being about video games, and did she think the violence was bad for her generation? Having never played much more than Tetris on a friend's Nintendo, she was not as prepared as she'd hoped to be for the question, but being as prepared as she was gave her the confidence to answer convincingly.

# SEVEN

# THE SELF-AWARE

## CASE STUDY: THE SELF-AWARE UNICORN

Lynsi Snyder became a billionaire on her thirty-fifth birthday. For this president and CEO of the West Coast fast-food chain In-N-Out Burger, being self-aware is a vital component of her success. It's what's helped her survive kidnapping attempts, got her through a difficult young adulthood of family deaths and failed marriages, and it is the not-so-secret secret to her company's success. In-N-Out has changed very little since her grandparents founded the burger chain in 1948.

"I really wanted to make sure that we stayed true to what we started with. That required me to become a protector," she said in a *Forbes* interview. That the menu hasn't significantly changed in seven decades is a testament to the brand's appeal. Few, simple items, served fresh via streamlined processes builds brand equity and an avid fan base. Snyder knows that happy customers are a product of happy employees, so wages have always been higher at In-N-Out versus other chains. Managers can expect salaries of $160,000 per year. This awareness and concern for her employees contributes to Snyder's annual appearance on Glassdoor's best bosses list.

The world has never been noisier or busier. Having the ability to be self-aware, to know weaknesses, to realize where you are in a crucial conversation is perhaps rarer than ever. Learning the process of self-awareness will cause you to stand out in a noisy, busy crowd.

When I was thirty-one years old, I was called to be the senior minister at the First Presbyterian Church of Houston. This was the church that Sam Houston attended, the oldest church in the city. And they just hired the youngest pastor on record.

I was in so far over my head. I didn't know all the things I didn't know. I wasn't lacking any self-confidence. Or to be more truthful, I wasn't lacking pride. And I wasn't lacking any vision, either. Okay, we can be more truthful here too: it wasn't vision; it was shiny object syndrome.

I had never run a large organization. I'd never been a senior minister of a large church. I hadn't even been a *member* of a large church. When I think back on it, if my search committee were evaluating thirty-one-year-old William for this job, we'd give him a constructive but certain pass.

One thing I *did* have going for me was that, because I was thirty-one, I knew everything.

Right?

## WHAT WE KNOW

Socrates didn't write much (if anything) down, but his most famous advice lives on as some of the best: "Know thyself." Those who are familiar with their strengths and weaknesses and who are honest with themselves are most likely to be Unicorns.

Self-awareness isn't just nice to have. Sure, it makes your life easier and the lives of anyone you interact with easier. How many of us wish houseguests were more self-aware when deciding how long to stay at our homes? Self-awareness, like so many of the traits Unicorns have, is a survival skill.

Think, once again, about our prehistoric ancestors. Who has a better chance at survival: the guy who *thinks* he can outrun a giant hyena or a guy who *knows* he can't? Being self-aware and knowing your limitations can save your life. While your overconfident buddy is out there trying—and failing—to be the fittest to survive, you can be safely ensconced up a tree, having clocked that beast and fled to safety, because you know you're no match for it.

### Self-awareness today

Being honest with themselves about their abilities helped your ancestors live long enough to produce the next generation. Today, these skills translate to success in your everyday life. When you're self-aware, you're not going to put yourself in danger or set yourself up for failure. Know that you are a zombie after an international flight? The Self-Aware will give themselves time to get acclimated, not commit to heading straight to the convention center to deliver the keynote address. Tend to sweat uncontrollably before important meetings? The Self-Aware know to wear black or another sweat-proof option, block out time to sit with the A/C on blast, and eliminate as much stress as possible before heading into the conference room. As for me, I can say, hand on heart, that I know myself well enough to not even get out of my seat if, at a Rockets game, my number is called to make a half-court shot for a large sum of money. It's never going to happen, and the cheerleaders should not even bother bringing out that giant foam core check.

On the positive side, knowing your strengths will allow you to position yourself for the win. Take Yankees pitcher and Hall of Famer Mariano Rivera. He could confidently jog onto the mound to pitch in the ninth because he was a closer. He knew he could protect the Yankees' lead. The team knew it too. That's playing to one's strengths.

The same thing happens for us normal humans too. I'm self-aware enough to know what is in my wheelhouse. One of my favorites? Speaking in public. I might not always feel calm, cool, and collected, but I usually am. And on the rare occasions I'm not, I can certainly play calm, cool, and collected on TV or anywhere else. Put me up in front of a crowd, and I'm happy to talk for as long as you'd like. It helps that I know the Bible chapter and verse and have had the good fortune to experience a lot in life. That's a lot of material I can draw from, and I'm self-aware enough to know that. My team knows it too. I've got a story for every situation, and no matter what the subject, I can always find a rabbit trail to bound down.

I'm not saying this to be arrogant. And you listing your strengths isn't arrogant, either. To know what you can confidently and capably do is essential to standing out.

We also know that being self-aware makes you better at finding solutions. Knowing yourself comes with a guaranteed pinch (or more) of humility, so when a self-aware person is faced with a challenge, they can decenter themselves from the issue. Being self-aware is knowing all about you while knowing that it's not all about you. Whatever the crisis, the Self-Aware remain even-keeled and committed to the goal. A great summary of how self-awareness can serve you in a crisis is the first few lines of Rudyard Kipling's "If." It's all about keeping calm while others are losing their heads. Unicorns can do what Kipling describes, thanks to self-awareness keeping them centered and grounded.

But it's not all stiff upper lips and colonialist grit. Self-aware people are generally happier too. The *Harvard Business Review* had a wonderful article on this very subject back in 2018 when, if you remember, "self-awareness" was starting to track as an industry buzzword. Turns out, according to their research, which built upon research published in 2004 in the *Journal of Social and Clinical Psychology* (what, you're not a subscriber?), self-awareness is the key to a lot of happiness. People who are self-aware are more creative, more effective at their jobs, better at relationships, better leaders, and more likely to be promoted. When it comes to knowing yourself, ignorance is not bliss.

## WHY HIRING MANAGERS LOVE THE SELF-AWARE

The less anyone has to tell you, the smoother things run. Hiring managers appreciate people who think about themselves in the way self-aware people do. They're less likely to take up unnecessary space in meetings, waste your time, or make others uncomfortable. When given constructive and genuine feedback, they'll take it to heart. Self-aware people are invaluable for company culture.

**Tips for cultivating self-awareness at work:**

- Ask people to be mindful of their habits in meetings: Do they talk over people? Do they talk for the sake of talking?
- Think about evaluations and ask team members to consider possible consequences of their feedback. Is the information they deliver truly helpful?

- Offer opportunities for constructive feedback, positive comments only, where teammates can share the good things they see in one another.

- Consider assigning tasks that play to employee strengths and preferences whenever possible. If John likes taking meeting notes, Steve is fine organizing the lunch order, and Hillary doesn't mind setting up the presentation slides, there's no reason to put them on a rotation where they're doing things they resent for any portion of the time. This is basically an example of 360 degrees of self-awareness, so bonus points if you achieve this one.

### WHO IS SELF-AWARE? DOLLY PARTON

I don't think anyone does self-aware better than Dolly. She took a bombastic image and made it her brand, synonymous with kindness, generosity, and empathy—not to mention amazing musical talent. She's often told the story of how, as a child, she idolized the style of a woman in town who did not have the best reputation. She said everyone else called the woman "cheap," but Dolly loved her big hair and tight clothes. In less enlightened times, Dolly has been criticized for the image she's cultivated, but no one can tell her anything she wasn't already aware of and isn't already perfectly happy with. "Discover who you are and do it on purpose," says Dolly Parton.

## WHAT WE'VE SEEN

When you think about it, we all benefit from other people's self-awareness. It's basically Emily Post's *Etiquette* in action. When someone moves over to make space for you on the subway, that's self-awareness. When someone could go on and on about a subject but doesn't because they know other people have places to go and things to do, that's self-awareness. When the tiny counter in the airplane bathroom has been wiped off, per the sign's suggestion, that's self-awareness.

Self-awareness is a pact we make with ourselves to be better for others.

### *Self-awareness serves ourselves too*

I'll never forget interviewing my friend Eric for a new position. We were doing a search for a very high-profile client, a very large organization in Southern California. I had messaged Eric to see if he was interested. A few days later, he messaged back and said, "You won't believe the story when I tell you."

So the next day, we got on the phone, and he told me how when I messaged him he was on a trip with his daughter. The trip was to

Southern California. Right before I had texted him to see if he was interested, his daughter asked him what he would be doing next in his career. He told her that he might keep doing his current job, might be asked to be CEO at another company, or that there was an outside chance he would decide to be a pastor somewhere else.

His daughter asked him what kind of church he would pastor if he decided that. He responded, "Well, it would have to be not in a major city but close to a major city. It would have to be a city that is going through some transition demographically. Because that's where I can best serve. And honestly, it would probably have to be near the coast. Because that's where Mom and I have been really happy."

Eric had been pastor in South Miami, in a wonderfully affluent community that was going through significant demographic changes. He did a fantastic job there. He was near the coast. He was outside a city but near a major city. Eric was self-aware enough to know the circumstances that would be right for him to take a job that he might not otherwise have considered. The job I was texting about? Near Los Angeles but not *in* Los Angeles. In a community that was affluent and going through significant demographic shifts. And finally . . . near the water, on a coast.

When he told me what he'd said to his daughter about where he saw himself, I was shocked. It showed a level of self-awareness that was rooted in his previous success and experience and his passion and his personal preference. That's pretty rare. And, unsurprisingly, Eric was a success again and has certainly proven to be a Unicorn standout.

### Report from the Unicorns

Of those surveyed, 8.38 percent identify themselves as strongest in the self-awareness category. This makes it the fourth most common of the traits. Self-awareness has benefited our Unicorns in a variety of ways, across all aspects of their lives.

*The Self-Aware create a better, more efficient culture and happier teams*

Unicorn Andrew E. has found that leaders with self-awareness are better leaders, better colleagues, and make better teams. "They create healthy work environments because they set the example and tone of how to lead, and they have their egos in check. In other words, they don't think they have it right all of the time, they ask for help, and they understand that they cannot do everything— sometimes they'll even suggest that their subordinates are better than them at something," he tells us.

On the other hand, he continues, "The leaders with no self-awareness, in my personal experience, have created toxic working environments, unhealthy staffs, and it is apparent that they themselves are unhealthy people. I have had self-aware leaders model humble and servant leadership, and those who are not self-aware model narcissism. Narcissists may find some success, but as soon as they leave, the mess they leave is revealed. I've seen it time and time again. Those who model self-aware leadership, their success has staying power because it's never about them."

Ralph K. says self-awareness is essential to building the best functioning teams. "Being self-aware allows me to identify what my strengths and weaknesses are—really what everybody's strengths and weaknesses are—to ensure everybody functions well together."

"You'll find that as a self-aware leader you will build better teams," concurs Adam Q. "You'll naturally fill in your blind spots and you'll be a humbler but more intelligent leader. Hand in hand with being self-aware comes the desire to know more profoundly your teammates and those you lead. By going deep with them you learn how to better respond to their reactions, how to identify their health, how to utilize their superpowers, how to show them appreciation effectively, and much, much more."

Unicorn Christine B. reminds us that the benefits of self-awareness aren't just anecdotal, they're canon. "I have an undergrad in leadership," she says. "And one of the facets they taught of being a good leader was self-awareness. Being self-aware has increased my communication skills and has also granted me knowledge of how to build a better team by filling in the areas that I am weak in or finding people who are better than me at those tasks."

## Self-aware enough for the job

Michael Z. has the benefit of time and many different calls to fine-tune his self-awareness: "I have been in ministry for over forty years and have served in nine churches. During this time I have had plenty of opportunities to try different things. I've learned as I've studied myself and received feedback from parishioners a good sense of what I do well *and* where my strengths are not. This has helped me as I've been interviewed by churches to be able to describe myself, my gifts, my ministry style, and how I approach situations. I've been able to say to churches, 'If you call me as your pastor, this is what you will get, and this is not what you'll see me trying to do.' As a pastor I am often a jack-of-all-trades, but I realize that there are some 'trades' that I'm better at than others."

Michael speaks as a pastor, but this is true of all job seekers. In the same way the Self-Aware are better at setting themselves up for success, they're better at knowing what will or will not be a good fit for them in the first place.

## Self-awareness for life

Like all of the twelve traits shared by Unicorns, self-awareness is just as critical for success in life as it is at work or in leadership. Josh P. puts it this way: "I have found that all of the twelve Unicorn qualities have helped me succeed in my work and life, but being self-aware has really been a whole different situation. I often ask myself, 'What is it like to work for me?' Or 'What is it like to have me as an employee or subordinate?' and 'What is it like to be married to me?'"

Scott W. says that knowing his weaknesses has helped him understand why he is the way he is and how to overcome them. "When faced with a decision, I tend to be slow to act, preferring to overanalyze and harvest as much information as possible trying to ensure that I won't take action that will embarrass me," he says. "Because I am aware of that tendency, I can push myself to action long before I feel fully educated on the subject (which previously would have meant 'far overeducated' on the subject). I push to action even when it feels painful. This has allowed me to move more quickly and to recognize that even when I make a mistake it isn't fatal. The benefits of acting more quickly far outweigh the risks of not feeling 100 percent comfortable."

And Jeff H. says that his self-awareness has led to greater understanding of the people around him. "It's not only being aware of your strengths and weaknesses but also understanding others' strengths and weaknesses and what triggers each," he says. This has helped him create a culture of love in both his professional and volunteer life. "Acceptance is not based on performance. Affirmation comes from doing the big stuff but also being aware of and recognizing when someone succeeds at the little stuff. This also creates a culture where correction can be healthy, producing change, not shame."

I've said before how the lack of ego that can come from self-awareness leads to better outcomes in the face of challenges. Manoj J. highlighted this very thing in the survey response, saying that being self-aware "offered insights into what I tend to do and why I tend to do certain things in a certain way. This awareness helps me be more productive and enables me to respond positively to tough situations and to more easily sail through the trouble."

**Fun fact:** President Theodore Roosevelt was a larger-than-life character, known for many acts of derring-do and idiosyncratic personality traits. Among the tamer of these were his long speeches and his pince-nez. In 1912, someone attempted to assassinate him, taking aim and shooting him as he was about to give a speech in Milwaukee, Wisconsin. Roosevelt was knocked backward but not killed. The bullet was stopped by the contents of his breast pocket: fifty folded pages of another long speech and the steel pince-nez case. With great self-awareness (and probably an unhealthy dose of adrenaline), Roosevelt got up, dusted himself off, and said, "It takes more than that to kill a bull moose."

## WHAT WE DO

Don't count on self-awareness magically appearing overnight; it takes a lifetime to perfect. Fortunately for us, it only takes an instant to get started on the path to a more self-aware you. The Unicorns show us how.

## Stay humble; be patient

You don't know what you don't know. Leave space for the possibility that you don't have it all figured out. Humility and vulnerability are your friends here.

Daniel B. tells it straight: "The key to being self-aware, in my opinion, is vulnerability."

Again, in an open-ended survey where respondents could— and did—write hundreds of words, Jacob B. took a similar tack to Daniel B. (no relation, I'm fairly sure): "Humility is the key to being self-aware."

For many of us, humility is learned the hard way. But these are the lessons that stick and make us better people. Michael L. is one of these people.

"During the early days of my ministry, I made a mistake with an older, retired (venerable) minister," he tells us. "Instead of listening to him and his ideas, I insisted on my own. When he pulled back from supporting me, I spoke to my mentor who helpfully gave me hard, but helpful, advice and criticism. I went back to the older minister, admitted my mistakes and shortcomings, and then closed my mouth and listened."

When you're vulnerable and humble, you're opening yourself up to the possibility that maybe you don't have it all figured out. This is a good thing. Especially as the Self-Aware are always reading the room and adjusting to their audience. As in: your take on airplane food might not be as well received in some situations as it is in others. Keep humble by keeping your audience and purpose in mind. These are superficial but important aspects of developing self-awareness.

Gregory S. says, "I am also aware that my strengths can become weaknesses depending on the circumstances, and I need to be aware of who I am speaking to or what project I am working on."

And then there's the gift of self-awareness that age brings. Mark C. explains: "I honestly think time and age have helped here. It wasn't always true, but at sixty I've been able to honestly recognize limits as well as gifts, giving thanks or making peace as each requires."

If all else fails, be patient. Self-awareness will find you.

## Trust others and ask

The fastest way to achieve better self-awareness is also the hardest. You have to trust others to tell you your blind spots. This isn't always easy, but it's worth it.

Not everyone is as lucky as Jason W., who didn't even have to ask to get constructive feedback that would help form his bolstered self-awareness. He had a wise-beyond-her-years wife and credits his growth in self-awareness to her. "In my early years, I was the poster child of 'knowing everything.' I didn't want to hear from anyone if I was doing something wrong or if there was a better way to do it."

(This hits home for yours truly, the former thirty-one-year-old parvenu with unfounded confidence for days.)

"Thankfully," continues Jason, "my young wife was gentle, patient, and direct in helping me 'grow up' and become humble."

Trust the ones who love you and care about your success to give you feedback that's helpful and sincere. And when you run out of their advice, turn to trusted friends and teammates.

Steve W. says if you want to know, you've got to ask: "I've learned that one of the hardest but most helpful questions to ask is,

'What is it like to be on the other side of me?' When I have gotten the courage to ask that of people I am in relationship with regularly (and when they have the courage to be honest with me), I have received a clarity of both strengths and weaknesses that I wouldn't have realized on my own."

Asking is hard but it's worth it, assures Nathan A. "I have spent a lot of time reading books and taking tests, but the most helpful piece in growing my self-awareness is asking people for feedback and listening to it. It is easy to get defensive, but listening to it and taking time to think about and process what I hear has been the best teacher."

Susan D. swears by her "ability to accept corrective criticism, asking the hard questions of other people about your own behavior and work habits."

She says, "I always ask employees, 'What can I do better?' I always want input. Learning to be self-aware also (I believe) removes my defensiveness (or maybe that comes with age). I always want to be a better manager, coworker, friend, parent, etc. The more you do it, the easier it becomes. It just becomes a natural part of your personality."

Adrian S. supports Susan's theory that it gets easier. "I make seeking feedback a life rhythm," he says. "Like breathing. I seek feedback more often than I eat."

Now, I wouldn't advocate forsaking food for feedback. Humans do not live by feedback alone, after all, but Adrian's devotion to asking the hard questions is part of what makes him a Unicorn.

He also has a great set of ground rules for asking and getting feedback.

Adrian S.'s rules of feedback engagement:

- You must be willing to risk looking insecure.

- Make it clear why you're asking. For example, "Asking for feedback like this is how I operate. I'm not unsure of myself; I just want to see what you see."
- Let people know they have your permission to give feedback and assure them you won't become defensive.
- Make sure your feedback givers know you won't always be acting on their advice.
- But at least occasionally, adjust based on their input.

### Know your limits . . . and know when to push them

As I said earlier in this chapter, knowing your limits is crucial to self-awareness. If one glass of celebratory prosecco at a work event hits you like a fifth of whiskey, avoid it. Likewise, if you know you get stressed right before a deadline, let your team know what to expect and plan accordingly. If you can practice being humble and asking for feedback, you will uncover your strengths and weaknesses quickly.

Megan C. has seen for herself the benefits of knowing her strengths: "Knowing your limitations is the easiest and most effective way to achieve your goals. When you overstretch and overtalk your ability to do something, you and your team will take the hit when the outcome doesn't line up with your words. It is better to commit and do well in three areas than to overcommit and have ten other areas of failure overshadow the three areas that you're actually good at. Be known for the things you do well and let that carry you for the long run."

And sometimes self-awareness is best found when you realize you need to outsource.

"I believe in the power of asking people to give me feedback. In the areas I can make changes, I do," says Aaron C. "But when changes are not possible, I commit to delegating those areas and empowering others to make improvements to the level required."

Laura T. also appreciates the gift of knowing when to focus on her areas of strength: "As I learned more about myself through leadership development, I realized that I needed to be aware of my strengths to maximize them. I also needed to know my weaker areas so that I could find others who were strong in those areas to create a team. Getting through life isn't about what I can do on my own but about what we can do together when we are 'self-aware with a common care.' There are practices that have helped me grow in my weaker areas, but ultimately I know I need to put my best energy into the areas [where] I excel."

The more you see that some things just aren't for you, and the more you see others nailing it, the more it reinforces your self-awareness.

Rich G. says this self-knowledge is essential to the effective running of his organization: "When I was younger I would get 'way out ahead of my skis.' I like that saying because it is accurate and telling. Sure, we all like to think we can do more, but I learned that once I accurately knew my capabilities without embellishments, we planned more accurately. Yes, you can always push yourself to do more, but you can't plan in a wish atmosphere."

This isn't to say our limits should be the borders that define us and for anything beyond them we should get someone else. Our limits should be a baseline. If you never want to get up in front of five thousand people and talk, that's fine. But being able to stretch and grow through your weak spots will pay off in the end.

As I'm writing this, it's the end of January and many of my team members are gung ho on various New Year's resolutions. One colleague has taken up running, which reminded me of back when I was first getting into long-distance running. It wasn't easy at first, but I knew my limit. Or, at least, my limit that day. Every day I went out for a run, I'd commit to making it one more streetlight. As I pounded the pavement of my neighborhood streets, I'd keep track of where I turned back the last time and push myself to go one more.

When you know your limits, you know how to push them. And that is how Unicorns get better. As Nathaniel P. sums it up, "Being self-aware puts you in a great place of growth."

Self-awareness is a lifelong journey, but don't forget that doing the work is worth it. Happiness comes with self-awareness, remember? Standout Scott M. has learned this: "I had to go through the tough process of learning about myself so that I not only could lead better but enjoy my life more, with the people I love."

## TAKEAWAYS TO BE AWARE OF

- Self-awareness is a social contract, benefiting you and those living in the world around you.
- Self-awareness leads to efficiency, better functioning teams, and happiness.
- Cultivate self-awareness by practicing humility and patience, trusting others to help, learning your limits, and pushing yourself to grow.
- Pince-nez and hard copy speeches save lives.

EIGHT

# THE CURIOUS

## CASE STUDY: THE CURIOUS UNICORN

Curiously enough, one of the most successful social entre-preneurs of all time started out as a mime. In college, Bill Rosenzweig was fascinated with the psychology of experi-ence. "What is it that can change people's minds and views? How do people have transformative experiences?" Such a major didn't exist at the time, so Rosenzweig combined theater (enter mime), film, and business to create his own course of study. This question never left his mind. After a transformative experience at a Japanese teahouse, fall-ing in love with the culture and values of tea, Rosenzweig began investigating a different kind of business model, one in which values were built into the framework of a company. "At that point, I was more of a want-repreneur than an en-trepreneur," he says. On a cross-country flight, Rosenzweig sat next to a man who looked "straight out of Banana Republic" because, it turned out, he was Mel Ziegler, founder of Banana Republic. They both asked for tea when the drinks cart came through and both were immediately put off by its bad taste and low quality. Rosenzweig let curiosity overcome his fear and said, "Why don't we start a tea company?" The two parted and began faxing each other about this new business. The faxes, from curious newcomer Rosenzweig to the Zen-like Ziegler, turned into a book called *The Republic of Tea* and became a master class in starting a values-based business. The Republic of Tea became a success. (The secret? Says Rosenzweig: have better tea.) Rosenzweig still uses his curiosity to invest in projects that help people transform for the better, sip by sip.

Steve Jobs once said, "Much of what I stumbled into by following my curiosity and intuition turned out to be priceless later on." Indeed, many of humanity's greatest minds, from Socrates to Einstein, celebrate curiosity as a key factor of success. But being curious is hard. We're not being offered potions to drink and rabbit holes to climb into at every turn, after all. And what's surrounding us on a regular basis is mundane. It's boring. Can we be expected to simply cultivate curiosity out of nothing?

Absolutely! You don't need to have curiosity thrust upon you. You can make your own. You can learn to find even the most prosaic interesting, ask questions, and listen to the answers with interest. This is what Unicorns do. I'll show you how.

## WHAT WE KNOW

"A person without curiosity may as well be dead," says Judy Blume. And it's true. As humans, we're wired to be curious. In fact, it's one of the best things about us. From the Clovis people of North America who got here by following that ice bridge in from Asia to those brave souls who literally and willingly launched themselves into space just to see what's there, curiosity is what we do and what we always have done.

"I think, at a child's birth, if a mother could ask a fairy godmother to endow it with the most useful gift, that gift would be curiosity," wrote Eleanor Roosevelt. I think she's correct that curiosity is the most useful gift—in the top twelve at least. But I also believe that all of us are born with curiosity, no fairy godmothers needed. While many of the other twelve traits of the Unicorns are learned over time, curiosity is one that comes as a factory setting.

*Curiosity doesn't make the world go round, but it's why we know what does*

Science is curiosity in action. Copernicus was curious about the earth's movement and if it just might be the case that we orbit the sun, ultimately coming up with what is still known as Copernican heliocentrism. Alexander Fleming was curious about the mold that killed the bacteria in his petri dish and discovered penicillin. Rachel Carson was suspicious of DDT's impact on the environment and started the modern conservation movement when she wrote *Silent Spring*. The list goes on.

Science is the obvious one. It's easy to see how science and curiosity pair up for the betterment of all humankind, but scientific discovery is not the only manifestation of curiosity. Curiosity is any time we take a genuine interest in someone, become absorbed with a show on the nature channel, or get caught up in our kid's research project to the point where they've long since gone to bed and we're doing a deep dive on the use of the portcullis in early medieval European fortress construction. It's not just science. Curiosity is looking around us and letting our brains be captivated.

*Curiosity is self-reinforcing and good for your brain*

Do you know why it feels so good to find out the answer to something you've been curious about? Dopamine. Our brains actually reward us for being curious and discovering the "why" of things. It's dopamine that gives us that buzzy feeling after we've looked up why it's called a binnacle list or what the name of those knicker-like golf pants are called. And who wouldn't want to chase that thrill again?

When our brains are primed for knowledge by curiosity in this way, we're also more likely to remember what kind of knowledge is inputted. This discovery is part of the reason why teachers allow students to follow their interests. That fourth-grade class might be doing their biography unit in language arts, but each kid is encouraged to research a person who is interesting to them. The outcomes demonstrate that we learn more, care more, and retain more when the subject is something we're curious about.

Research has also shown that curiosity is good for your mental health. Anxiety, for example, is not compatible with the feel-good, mental high-fiving your brain does when you're wondering and discovering. Beyond that, the simple act of being curious about something that isn't yourself can put you in a better mental state. Checking in on a friend or loved one who might also be going through an anxious or difficult time can be enough to derail your own anxiety and give you a dopamine boost from satisfied curiosity.

It's not always easy to remember to be curious. Life gets in the way. A lot. But as much as you can, follow the advice of author Clarissa Pinkola Estés when she says, "Practice listening to your intuition, your inner voice; ask questions; be curious; see what you see; hear what you hear. . . . These intuitive powers were given to your soul at birth."

**Fun fact:** Throughout his life, Rudyard Kipling maintained his curiosity with a good deal of his own exploration. He was born in India and would live in various locations there as well as in the US and the UK. He also traveled extensively to Japan and other Asian locales. He had more opportunities and privilege than most folks, and at times he reflected contemporary colonialist belief systems. Kipling was by no means perfect, but his way of showing us the world was inspired.

## WHY HIRING MANAGERS LOVE THE CURIOUS

When a candidate is curious, it suggests genuine engagement with your company and interest beyond a paycheck. Curiosity is a great way to predict if a candidate will be willing to learn and grow in their position as well.

**Tips for cultivating curiosity at work:**

- Give time and budget to team members who want to learn more about a particular subject or skill.
- When challenges come up, practice asking questions before throwing out solutions.

> • Take time to get to know your team members on a more personal level by offering optional team lunches and other experiences.

## WHAT WE'VE SEEN

We are all born curious. That's the best foundation you can get. The struggle, however, comes from growing up, learning more, and pushing curiosity to the side. Getting your childlike sense of wonder and discovery is easy. Keeping it is hard.

If you're paying any attention at all, you can tell fairly quickly if the person you're engaging with has kept their curiosity, or if they let a dull, dreary workaday world drive it out of them.

*Some of the Curious shine brighter than others because some of the Curious are Unicorns*

During my time as senior pastor at First Presbyterian Church of Houston, one of our congregants was Senator Lloyd Bentsen. He served as the secretary of the treasury for President Clinton. When Senator Bentsen died, I was asked to perform the funeral service. Right before I was to speak, the family asked if someone could give a eulogy. And in arguably the shortest straw ever drawn in public speaking, I ended up having to follow a eulogy by President Clinton.

Before the funeral service, we had a small private graveside service for family and close colleagues. We scheduled some time after the graveside and before the main funeral service for family, friends, and colleagues from Washington to visit. But as luck would have it, the heavens opened and the rains came down in a torrential downpour. We had to move everybody back to the church, to join a large public reception before the main funeral service. In order to keep President Clinton from having to meet with all of the crowds—and to avoid the security risk that presented—I was asked if he could sit in my office with me until the service started. We ended up together for quite a long time.

When we got to my office, I tried to ask President Clinton questions about himself. I figured he would like to talk about himself. Most people do . . .

But he, like nearly every super successful person I have been around, insisted on turning the conversation back to me.

I asked President Clinton a question about himself. He pointed over to a brochure on my desk and asked, "Are you leading a trip to Greece? You should really meet my friend who works for the Greek Orthodox Church."

I was tempted to chuckle and reply, "Sure, I'll just google his contact information, Mr. President."

I switched the conversation and asked him about a yarn bracelet he was wearing on his wrist. I said I recognized it. He told me it was from children in an under-resourced country that he learned about and proceeded to ask me how I knew about it. I told him I knew some folks doing relief work in the area. Again, he told me that I must get to know one of his friends there.

No matter how much I tried to turn the conversation toward him, he always deftly turned the conversation back to me. It made me feel as if I were the only person in the room. And irrespective of how anyone is persuaded politically, I left that meeting understanding why people voted for him.

That's the power of curiosity.

## *Why it pays to be curious*

Basketball coach Phil Jackson was once asked his secret for coaching so well. He simply said, "I listen." In our new world of people doing everything they can to promote themselves as smartest, strongest, and best, very few people work on learning to listen to people. But doing so is an essential tool in the standout toolbox of skills.

Of our survey respondents, 7.5 percent identify as curious dominant. Like President Clinton, they ask; and like Coach Jackson, they listen. And like most Unicorns, they succeed.

## *Curiosity gets you in the door and takes you further*

A trend in interviewing these days is to ask a candidate what they're reading, watching, or, in short, curious about. I think this is a great tactic, and standout Max W. swears by this question. "I find that people who have a healthy and vibrant curiosity can easily speak to what they are curious about," he says. "It really does not seem to matter what that is, just that they have curiosity. I've found they tend to make the best team members and the most productive employees."

A friend of ours, Alyssa, once described her early days as a marketing professional. She worked for a small, niche agency in the suburbs. It was run by . . . well, let's just say the opposite of curious people. The anticurious. She was young, inexperienced, and overly deferential to this group who did not deserve her respect.

"I wanted to do things right and wasn't given a whole lot of direction," she told me. "So I asked questions. Apparently a lot of questions. Too many for them, anyway. I always tried to be considerate of their time, so I'd pop my head into my boss's office when she wasn't busy, and I'd ask if she had a second for a quick question. I thought I was doing the right thing. But I came in one day to find the whole office plastered with photos of me from my Facebook page. I had a speech bubble above my head reading, 'Umm, quick question!' My boss had done it after I'd left the night before. She thought it was hilarious. I was humiliated. The owner of the company was standing there too. He saw my flustered face, twisting to keep from crying from shame, and told me that I was allowed to smile. It was funny, he said. I realized then and there that this wasn't my place, and these weren't my people."

But sometimes you do find your people and your curiosity, and questions are seen for what they are: signs of your strengths and desire to improve. Standout Emilie M. found more kindness and support in the US Navy than Alyssa experienced at a Midwest marketing agency.

"As a senior leader in the US Navy in a new position, I realized that I had a lot to learn in order to be effective and to achieve the knowledge level and competence of most of my peers," Emilie M. says. "I asked questions about everything all the time. My supervisor chuckled one day and called me 'in a constant state of professional curiosity.' I thought he might be irritated by all my questions, but instead he affirmed that this was actually a critical trait to success and ongoing professional growth."

Max W. found that following his curiosity led to finding likeminded people who could help his organization thrive. "I found a group of peers who were all forming conclusions around the same ideas I was researching. We began to feed off of one another, and some really cool and innovative leadership models emerged. I not only found benefit in all of that process and application, but it also helped me to appreciate where following my curiosity might lead. I honestly can't think of a single example of where following curiosity was like a waste of time."

## Curiosity keeps you humble

Emilie M. found that being curious keeps her humble, helping her see the humanity in others: "The idea is to stop seeing them as an irritant or obstacle and use curiosity to uncover their needs, objectives, and challenges. It works. I've learned to leverage curiosity as a sort of superpower. Whether professionally or personally, I've found it to be a necessary leadership trait."

Travis M. says this curious approach to people makes you a better leader: "We are constantly learning from others, and one way to do that is to be curious. Even if you do not agree with someone, you can be curious about what and why they believe what they do. Being curious needs to be embraced because curiosity does not always kill the cat. In fact, more often than not curiosity breeds empathy and humility, two traits that make a good leader."

Choosing curiosity is something Tim S. strives for. "I believe curiosity is both a choice and a skill that requires practice. I have made the choice to remain curious about people so that I can listen to them in a better way. It isn't just that someone holds a certain view. You have to ask why they hold it. 'What experiences have shaped them? What stress are they carrying that I don't know about?' It helps me notice things I didn't notice before and to be less defensive and combative."

As is the case for many other of our twelve characteristics, humility is just under the surface, helping our Unicorns find shared humanity and be better, more empathetic people.

**WHO IS CURIOUS? TREVOR NOAH**

Noah is the former host of *The Daily Show*, a busy enough gig, but even during his seven-year run hosting the show, he found time to do stand-up, which is his first love. He's been lauded as an "incredible observer," which makes not only his comedy sharp but his interviews as well. Nothing gets by Noah, who seems to have been born, among other things, both curious and inspired to use his gifts to help people see beyond their own point of view.

## WHAT WE DO

Albert Einstein was the poster child for curiosity, telling *LIFE* magazine in 1955, "The important thing is not to stop questioning. . . . One cannot help but be in awe when he contemplates the mysteries of eternity, of life, of the marvelous structure of reality. It is enough if one tries merely to comprehend a little of this mystery each day."

I wouldn't put what I do with my curiosity in quite such an elegant way, but I am a naturally curious person. I've been fortunate to be able to act on my curiosity to the fullest. Most recently, inspired by the trip I took to New Zealand wine country, I've decided to learn more about wine and have been taking sommelier classes. You can take the man out of Hawke's Bay, but you can't take the Hawke's Bay out of the man.

### Keep informed

Unicorns stay informed intentionally. Bo W. says, "I read a book a week minimally, often two. I supplement this with newspapers or articles from other countries and an app that summarizes nonfiction books for leaders. Getting input from outside the United States as well as long-form and short-form reading helps me see things from different angles. I watch movies or programs, but I don't watch television. Once the program is over, I turn off the television. So even what I watch during the week is planned and not a tool used to 'numb out.'"

Curiosity isn't a spectator sport, Shane R. says. "To be curious, one needs to take time to be informed. I work hard on the latter, starting my day with an executive briefing using AI feeds that give me clear, precise, and informative data. From there, I can extrapolate what is relevant and important and what action may be required. Staying curious is an action, not a position."

Pamela L. reminds us that staying informed can also mean looking inward and digging deeper into issues close to home. She says, "The tip I would offer is to pay attention more carefully when a question keeps niggling in the back of your mind when you are faced with a dilemma, decision, or roadblock. Write the question down and ask it several ways. Often, leaders ignore the right question because deep inside they are afraid to open Pandora's box. It's by opening the box that authentic, creative solutions come."

### Stay humble

Once again, humility is your friend. Being curious requires the same kind of humility that being self-aware does. Remember that you don't know everything. Proceed accordingly.

"You need humility if you're going to be curious," says Shane R. "You need it to learn new thoughts, concepts, and ideas. As for me, I am constantly curious to see how others succeed and manage their productivity; what tools, approaches, and systems do they use? I encourage anyone working to achieve organizational and personal success to be a humble inquisitor on their journey."

"Don't be so certain of your own opinions, takes, studies, or outlook," cautions Dylan O. "In order to understand people and things more deeply, suspend judgment, be tolerant, and lean forward instead of digging in. Try to understand differences and mend them. Not only will things go better for you, but you will find genuine beauty and fuller truth."

Some of us learn humility and some of us have humility thrust upon us. Sarah F. says, "Graduate school was a humbling experience. But once I realized that I do not have the market cornered on truth and experience, I found that being curiously interested in others promoted conversation as well as innovation. Everyone has something to offer."

## Ask and listen

Every part of being curious can boil down to this: asking and listening. Almost 90 percent of the 7.8 percent of Unicorns who consider curiosity their best strength listed "listening" in their survey responses.

Ask any question of any person. You'll find there is no such thing as a boring person. There is no situation you can't learn from. English newspaper columnist Caitlin Moran gives this advice: "Whenever you can't think of something to say in a conversation, ask questions instead. Even if you're next to a man who collects pre-seventies screws and bolts, you will probably never have an opportunity to find out so much about pre-seventies screws and bolts, and you never know when it will be useful."

This philosophy is a great way to keep curious. Unicorns have so much to say about asking the right questions and listening with purpose.

Julianna C. says, "Active listening was a tool I discovered in a college course in my thirties. Pairing this style of listening with my natural bent of curiosity, I ask lots of questions, questions other people usually don't think to ask. But asking good questions has taken practice, and I have used various exercises and opportunities for development. Curiosity is a skill worth growing in, so my tip is to evaluate your ability to stay curious, ask good questions, and actively listen to others. And don't forget to practice."

"Listen, don't just hear," urges Lisa C. "It took me years to realize that tasks are important, but people matter more. Spend time (even when it's messy and inconvenient) with broken people who want to be heard and affirmed. Don't listen just to have an answer or be a 'fixer.'"

Curiosity is caring, says Tonia B. "Care about others and practice asking about them. Think of others first."

Lisa S. says, "Listen instead of talking. Ask questions instead of giving opinions. Ask why. And ask why a lot. Everybody has a story. I want to hear it."

## CURIOUS TAKEAWAYS

- Being curious about others is good for business and your brain.
- Curiosity yields humility and solutions.
- Find something you love and learn more, even if it's just for your own personal enjoyment.
- Ask questions and listen.

## NINE

# THE CONNECTED

## CASE STUDY: THE CONNECTED UNICORN

"Success in any field, but especially in business, is about working with people, not against them," writes Keith Ferrazzi. The best-selling author and entrepreneur has helped the world realize the power of connection, not only for one's personal advancement but for the betterment of everyone. The son of a Pittsburgh steelworker at a time when the steel industry was failing, Ferrazzi saw the disconnect between his father's experience and the boss's actions. His father had ideas for helping the company turn around, but management didn't talk to workers. That night around the dinner table, says Ferrazzi, he decided to commit his life to helping families like his. He would grow up and help save jobs. The way to do this, he discovered, was by creating connections. If more teams were truly functional, people and businesses would thrive.

To get to where he is today, Ferrazzi himself had to make the right connections. And he did. His parents weren't well-off, but they were committed to education. Ferrazzi took advantage of every opportunity school afforded him. He made genuine connections with his professors. He worked hard for and landed an internship at Deloitte. He went above and beyond every chance he saw, including approaching the Deloitte CEO and asking to take on extra projects. Within three years of graduating business school, Ferrazzi became the company's CMO. Making meaningful relationships with a variety of different people along the way has enabled Ferrazzi to successfully and lucratively preach what he's always practiced: connection.

Most people didn't see the 1993 Michael J. Fox movie *For Love or Money*. The small percentage of us who have and somehow remember it to this day can tell you that the film is all about connections. The main character is Doug, a hotel concierge at a fancy, fictional New York City hotel. Although he's driven, tough, and a bit morally circumspect, he's played by Michael J. Fox, so he has a heart of gold. Throughout the movie, Doug, who dreams of opening his own hotel someday, wheels and deals, making magical experiences for his guests, always seeming to know just what they need when they need it. He is on a first-name basis with the saleswomen at Tiffany, arranges hairdresser appointments for desperate Midwestern wives, and has access to VIP seating at the Rainbow Room. And when it seems like Doug's chances of having a hotel of his own have gone up in flames, the day is saved, thanks to the kindness he showed people he never expected repayment from.

In short: it's always been about who you know. Connections are king, especially when it comes to getting ahead. But instead of smoke-filled rooms and whom your father went to college with, I want you to think of connections as relationships you can build from anywhere. Being connected is about more than what powerful and influential people you can network with. It's about being a good person to all people because you never know where your life may lead.

## WHAT WE KNOW

Behind every great success story is an element of luck, of being in the right place at the right time. The place and time are important, for sure, but who happens to be there might matter even more. Examples abound of people connecting at just the right time. Harrison Ford was hired to help with auditions for *Star Wars*, reading lines with hopeful actors, only to land the part of Han Solo himself.

Anne Sullivan's life was saved by connections: having suffered from poor eyesight since she was a child, she took her chance when she could. When an inspector came to investigate the brutal workhouse/orphanage she'd been sent to, she seized the opportunity and begged him to send her to the Perkins School for the Blind. A few months later her wish was granted. From there, she was able to graduate as valedictorian of her class. Shortly thereafter, the school suggested her for the job of tutoring seven-year-old Hellen Keller.

And then there's one of my favorites, Moses. His story is a monument to who you know—from the Egyptian princess who found him in the basket to his sister poised and ready to suggest his mom as a caretaker to, well, God Himself. The story of Moses wouldn't endure to this day if he'd been found by just any random person hanging out by the Nile and if God hadn't invested in him as a connection.

### Connecting: it gets the job

Experts estimate that between 75 and 80 percent of jobs are won thanks to personal or professional connection. Networking is more important than ever. We can think of this in terms of the rarefied air of the Soho House in any given major city, where the rich and connected get richer and more connected, or any other institution like this that has existed as long as capitalism has.

Class mobility (and lack thereof) is an underlying theme of so many classic novels. From Dickens and Thomas Hardy to Tolstoy and Dostoevsky, these writers tell us just how hard it is to get ahead if you're not born ahead. Servants have servant parents and will have children who become servants. The rich stay rich. Meaningful connection with someone outside a character's class happens rarely, but when it does, it usually signals the turning point of a character's life. Suddenly a poorer person has a chance at something better.

Fortunately, the world has opened up a bit more, and while it's arguably still preferable to be born into a connected family and position in society, the playing field isn't as uneven as it once was. We can thank the internet for this. Suddenly, those who want to connect can do so, on a smorgasbord of platforms designed for that very thing. LinkedIn not only tells us who might be a good connection; it tells us why and what we have in common. There's a layer of trust built in, so all we have to do is click a button to connect. It's still very much a world of "who you know," but now more of us can know people we would otherwise have never met.

But knowing people isn't always enough. You can be in the same room as someone or be "friends" on all the social platforms, but if you can't connect on a human level, you're not going to succeed. For that reason, there are programs that help kids, who might not otherwise have the opportunity, get access to the tools that will help them connect on a human level. AVID is a program in many public high schools that helps identify potential first-generation college students. It provides them extra support plus teaches life skills that help open doors.

The Blue Water Foundation in San Francisco and SailFuture in Florida teach sailing to underserved youth. New York's Metropolitan Golf Association offers free clinics and programs specifically for kids who wouldn't otherwise have access to the game. Critics of such programs scoff and say teaching underprivileged kids country club sports is ridiculous. But Unicorns know how important skills like these (and the confidence that come with them) are. They're a way to convert "connection" into "social capital," aka, the art of making connection work for your benefit.

## Social capital makes the world go round

Remember my impromptu meeting with the curious President Clinton? Well, his connections certainly helped me. I appreciated his telling me that I really should connect with his various important friends, but I never thought anything would come of it. He's charismatic and curious, but also pretty busy. So I didn't think about it again until a week later when I got a call from the office of the archbishop of Constantinople, asking about my trip and if there was anything I needed. The next week I got a letter from the ambassador to Bolivia asking about our missions. Finally, a couple of weeks later, I was sent a copy of President Clinton's autobiography with a handwritten note accompanying it.

Unicorns all have a story like this one. Maybe not on a presidential level, but the connection is the key.

David M. says he learned this at an early age: "My grandfather taught me early on that if you don't ask, the answer will always be no. As I developed into a leader, I realized that you'll get a lot more yeses than noes if you have deep, solid relationships and connections. I go out of my way to build those relationships."

Another Dave, this time Dave F., views his connections as opportunities to strengthen his own team and to help others. "I learned a long time ago that I don't have to be the smartest, strongest, fastest, etc. But knowing and teaming up with those people can bring about great, important outcomes," he says. Over the years, Dave has been able to plumb his circle and connect them with one another, confident that they would do the same for him. "I don't look at people I meet as potential resources but instead try to find out who they are and what their focus is, and if doors open, I make a note of what that person knows, how I might nurture that relationship or friendship. . . . I've come to know a number of people over the years, and I feel confident that if someone came to me looking for anything from filling a position or finding someone with an area of expertise, I might well be able to help. Equally, I believe that a great many of the people I've met over the years would give an honest attempt at assisting me in the same way."

### Being connected keeps you connected

Getting connected is key, but staying connected is where you become invaluable. Now, I'm as confident as I can be in my marriage. Adrienne and I are a team, and we're proud of the family and life that we've built based on our love and respect for each other. Even so, a little extra insurance never hurt anyone, right?

Adrienne's family has the best recipe for gumbo. It's the featured dish at all of the family gatherings. It's incredible and everyone loves it. More than jewelry or other family heirlooms, this gumbo recipe is treasured. But there was a problem. The only person who knew the secret recipe was Adrienne's grandmother. When she is no longer with us on earth, what's the family going to do?

Luckily, I knew a guy. Me. I was able to persuade Adrienne's grandmother to teach me the recipe so it's safe for future generations. And if that makes me a little bit more valuable to that side of the family, well then I consider myself lucky I could connect with and learn from the matriarch.

**Fun fact:** "Six degrees of separation" is the idea that every human on earth can be connected to each other by six or fewer acquaintances. In 1994, three college students invented "Six degrees of Kevin Bacon," the idea that everyone in Hollywood is connected to Kevin Bacon by six or fewer film roles.

### WHO IS WELL CONNECTED? GLENNON DOYLE

Doyle began as a mommy blogger and has since turned her ability to connect with people on a computer screen into an empowerment empire. From very public breakups and breakdowns to a podcast and three *New York Times* bestsellers, Doyle has become beloved by so many for her warmth, vulnerability, and inspiring words. She's also put her platform to good use. She's founded a nonprofit called Together Rising

that transforms "collective heartbreak into effective action."
People all over the world donate a maximum of twenty-five
dollars to this cause, most recently for causes like reuniting
families separated by political conflict. At the same time,
Doyle makes frequent appearances (with other celebrity
friends) on the *Together Live Tour*, a storytelling event aimed
at connecting communities.

## WHAT WE'VE SEEN

In business, being well connected is more than half the battle. We
owe a big part of the success of Vanderbloemen to connections on
social media. I know it sounds silly, but it's true: when we started,
I'd already had fifteen years of making really odd and diverse connections. It was also when social media was going mainstream.
Early adoption of social media, along with my diverse network and
connections there, allowed us to be at the "right place, right time."
This attracted a way bigger audience than we would have been able
to gain by traditional methods. Connections trumped establishment.
We were new and had no reputation to speak of, but we were visible,
and we had connections to amplify our mission.

You could say I grew this diverse network of mine the old-
fashioned way: on the golf course. Part of the reason I get excited
about those programs that give kids access to golf is because I know
just how important golf is to my success. The connections I made
there are the reason I am where I am today.

## *Report from the Unicorns*

Of those surveyed, 6.88 percent identified most with the Connected. The Unicorns cite a lot of reasons why being connected is the key to their success.

### BEING CONNECTED ENABLES YOU TO LEARN FROM THE BEST

When "the best" aren't anywhere to be found, you sometimes have to seek them out. That's what Jennifer G. discovered at an early age. Knowing whom you can learn from is important, she says. "Growing up with divorced parents, I had to learn many firsts to navigate on my own. Many of those experiences didn't go so well, and I learned quickly to look around and find others who have been successful at the things I wanted to succeed in," she says. "I made an effort to connect with them, to see if I could build rapport with them. Where I was able, I asked them to mentor me. Learning from those who were successful in the things I valued is a skill I have found very helpful."

### BUILDING BETTER LEADERS AND TEAMS

You're probably detecting a theme here by now. All twelve of the standout traits can help you become a better leader. Here's why being connected helps.

Dan S. says when your team knows that you care, you'll do better: "I'm a big believer in social capital and the need to bank credit with members of my team before I can spend it. In my experience, team members respond more readily to a leader they like and respect, and who they know cares about them. Establishing rapport drives loyalty and commitment among all members of the team, especially the leadership."

Lief A. agrees, adding that a strong connection with your team is the foundation of its success: "Building relational capital is one of the first things I work on when starting in a role. It is a lot easier to get buy-in or be included in decision-making processes if you've already established those relationships up and down the org chart."

"I invest in relationships of key leaders and everyone on the team," says Ben C. "I believe relational equity is the fuel that helps push the mission and allows us to do it in the context of community so people feel valued and like they're part of something special. All this tends to make everyone work harder, trust me more, value my input, trust my corrections, buy into our vision, and want to be on the team."

"I build relationships with people in every aspect of my work. I know that when I am well-connected, I am well advantaged in terms of work and delivery," adds Martin W.

But this book isn't only about building great teams, being the best leader, and thriving in your professional life. Unicorns stand out because of their qualities as a whole, how they relate to the world, not just the office. Being connected helps you see that people are more alike than different. When you can truly connect with others, you can appreciate our shared humanity. And you become a better person.

For Doug I., an essential part of connecting is discovering how he can help. "When I connect with people, I begin to see them as an opportunity to serve. The task is important, but the relationships I have with the people I work with are more valuable to me."

Charles M. brings us full circle, back to our Michael J. Fox movie reference, when he reminds us that, no matter our title, we all need the same things, we are all valuable, and we all deserve to be treated with respect. "I've learned that no matter how high up a person is, they still wanted to be acknowledged as an individual with feelings and ideas, and as someone who mattered," he says. "Looking past the position to the individual helps break down any walls that may be up on either side. I have personal relationships with pastors of megachurches, authors, people of influence, executive directors of state conventions, farmers, cashiers, and waiters. I have been gifted with the ability to connect with all kinds of people, and I treat everyone with the same respect no matter what."

"I tell people that the best investment is in people," says Thomas C. "At the end of the day, it is those trust relationships and people you poured into who will take care of you and keep you living abundantly and generously."

## THE CONNECTED HAVE MORE FUN

A lot of the time, it's just more fun to be connected. Spencer P. tells us how he learned this . . . eventually. "I used to think it was much easier and faster to just do the work myself," he says. "But this can easily lead to arrogance when you succeed or despair when you fail. Since then, I've worked hard to know my weaknesses and bring people around me who are strong in those areas. While this does take time and energy, it has brought more joy and meaning as I've deepened relationships with my teams. Additionally I've seen over the decades that investing in relationships with people pays huge dividends in the future."

Dividends, says Spencer, such as laughter, snacks, and endurance. "We have many of our meetings in people's homes when possible. We eat snacks and catch up with one another. We value laughter and honesty and fun and sharing one another's personal and spiritual burdens. While all this also takes time and energy (we often don't actually start a meeting until twenty minutes in), it helps immensely when we have conflict. Because we like and enjoy one another, because we've built relationships with one another, because we see one another as family, when conflict and challenges and disagreement arise we are able to get through them in a healthy way. Tough stuff will always come, but if you've built connections based on community, trust, and love you will more often than not be able to endure that storm."

## WHY HIRING MANAGERS LOVE THE CONNECTED

The more endorsements a candidate has, the better! Hiring managers possess better-than-average judgment of character, but even they appreciate more people vouching for a candidate. Even better, when a position opens up, they can always rely on the Connected to spread the word and get good names in the ring.

**Tips for cultivating connection at work:**

- Offer referral bonuses for team members who recommend good candidates.
- Encourage networking; give team members allowances for professional memberships and conference attendance.
- Mentor, mentor, mentor. Says Unicorn Cathy H., "By taking the time to get to know the people I work with and lead, I have built deep, lasting relationships. These have led to opportunities to mentor others in their careers. I feel I have made—and continue to make—a lasting

impact in their lives. With one younger staff member, I invested time in unearthing her strengths and then finding ways to tweak her job to capitalize on those strengths. I also brought her along to leadership opportunities and invited her to travel to Kenya with me. This investment has led to personal and career growth for her, as well as a lasting friendship with her."

## WHAT WE DO

"Only connect," writes E. M. Forster in *Howards End*. This has been interpreted as an entreaty to align thoughts and feelings—head and heart—as the way to achieve passion and purpose and to reach our loving, human potential.

Unicorn Jordan W. echoes this sentiment and tells us how to put it into practice: "Always notice others. Meet them where they are, walk with them; help them realize their gifts and strengths and grow in their journey. Love them."

Not all of the Connected put it as plainly as Jordan W. does. But when it comes to more tactical practices for growing your connections, strong themes emerge.

### Go for quality and quantity

Also in *Howards End*, the main character, Margaret, observes: "The more people one knows the easier it becomes to replace them. . . . It's one of the curses of London." Swap "London" with "the internet," and she's summed up our modern life. The more connections you have, the easier it is to devalue them.

This would suggest that choosing quality connections is better than gathering a large quantity of them. But I would argue that it doesn't have to be either/or, thanks to the same reason we're asked to choose in the first place: the internet. Social media makes it easy to connect, while also making it fairly easy to grow your connections. It just takes a little discipline.

"We live in the most connected times the world has ever known, yet few people are intentional about it," says Chris H. He argues that putting time and effort into your online connections yields quality and quantity. "I have developed a network of nearly ten thousand connections on LinkedIn and Twitter, communicating with many of those connections often."

Chris H. gives us two practical suggestions for making this work:

1. Use the search feature on Twitter/LinkedIn to find like-minded professionals in your industry. When you find them, connect with them, and thank them for connecting with you. "I have been able to harvest great ideas, connect great people to each other, and deepen my sense of a truly global network of professionals in my area of expertise," he says.

2. When someone who has connected with you on social media asks to connect with you on the phone or on Zoom, don't delay; connect with them as soon as you can. "Those conversations of getting to know each other and swapping ideas are priceless," he says. "You can truly develop meaningful friendships with people this way."

Brad L. makes the point that there's no such thing as "quality versus quantity" when it comes to the time and energy you put into making connections. "Quality versus quantity is a false dichotomy when it comes to time spent building relationships," he argues. If you are genuine and intentional, any amount of connecting counts. "Spending time with people builds trust and credibility, which leads to relational capital, which can be spent when it matters most. If you actually care about people, this will come naturally," he says.

Caring about people and taking an interest can't be undersold when we're talking about connection. "If people know that you are 'for' them and care about their interests, they will go the extra mile. So I make sure to ask questions about family and other interests as much as possible," reports Unicorn Jonny W.

Debra C. agrees: "The best way to build teams is through relationships. The best way to build relationships is through investing in others, sincerely caring for and engaging in the lives of others."

Caring about others isn't just a strategic thing to do; it's the human thing to do.

### Look for cracked doors

Connections aren't always spontaneous. You must seize your opportunities.

Tom C. suggests: "Prepare for any conversation to be an opportunity to connect someone to someone else. Keep notes on people and what they do because you might be the link that connects the person you just met with someone who can help them accomplish their destiny and purpose. For example, at a conference recently I met the CEO of an organization that has a presence in multiple countries. They were looking to expand their impact by addressing human trafficking, but they needed to connect with an organization that could help them do that. At the end of our conversation, I had given them a couple of names and contact information of people who could potentially meet their needs. With these connections, the CEO has expanded the organization's impact, helping people that they would not have been able to reach before."

Paul T. agrees with the power of a conversation. "Opportunities are just a conversation and connection away. These are key for opening doors so that vision and mission can be shared, and for establishing mutually beneficial relationships."

And don't forget to keep at it. Being a Unicorn isn't about things falling into place at every turn. It's about having the tenacity to keep going. As Ben S. advises, "Always seek an additional connection in all situations. When you hear 'no,' think of it instead as a 'not yet.'"

## Do the work

It's like the old adage tells us: the harder I work, the luckier I get.

Those who are willing to put in the effort will be better connected than those who leave it to chance.

DeAnna S. reminds us that part of doing the work means doing the homework and being willing to learn. "Life is all about building effective and lasting relationships personally and professionally. Learning from different cultures and ethnic groups has expanded my knowledge and understanding of people, helping me to better approach challenges and find solutions."

It can also be beneficial to cast a wide net in a strategic way. Andrew B. suggests plugging into networks that align with your passions, especially on a local level. And if you don't have a lot of bandwidth for this, work smarter, not harder: "If you don't have time to create a new network or program every time you get interested in something, it's helpful to meet your chamber of commerce, your local school leadership, and your local government. When my organization set a goal to be more involved with supporting the community, I attended a countywide coalition for agencies, nonprofits, businesses, and churches that focused exclusively on helping families experiencing poverty. Through those relationships, my team and I were able to build a sustainable presence in the community. It also helped us establish mutually beneficial relationships outside our organization."

Above all, David B. reminds us to keep our eye on the prize in terms of why you're doing the work to connect: "Always begin with the end in mind. Develop your vision and work backward. Don't be afraid to delegate, and keep the momentum."

### Give more than you take, and follow through

Being connected can be a big liability if you're not mindful of the way you behave in the world. Conrad W. tells us, "I've learned to give more than I take; this is how investing in people works. If you develop a reputation for being a taker, you'll soon have no connections, and your reputation will precede you. People talk. But if you choose to give, your generosity creates buzz and enables you to make connections you may not otherwise have access to."

This is a philosophy rooted in a strong sense of morality, Conrad W. continues. "It's about integrity," he says. "If you say you can do something, do it. And do it well. There's no faster way to burn a bridge to a strategic connection than failing to follow through."

Will M. seconds this: "Never burn bridges. You never know when you're going to experience a situation where a person from your past would be an ideal fit. You don't want to have burned a bridge with that person. I got my current position thanks to a person I helped hire in my past job. They gave me the recommendation for this job, and I could not be happier."

## *Pay it forward*

While you're being careful to protect your future by keeping bridges structurally sound, it's just as important to think of others' futures. Standout John H. is very aware of the good he can do for others with his connections, having experienced it himself. He says, "I don't keep my connections to myself. I try to connect others to the friends I have, and I use my influence to help others connect to further their goals. I learned this from a person who 'invited me into the room' and gave me an opportunity when I needed it."

Pastor Corey G. considers this a moral imperative: "Recognizing that building people is the most important thing we'll ever have the chance to do is essential. No matter what you or your company produces, the only thing that will last forever is people and relationships with those people. When we recognize the value of people, we begin to recognize the value of the work we do."

Life isn't a straight line. It's a spiral. While you're climbing the mountain of success, don't forget to keep the path clear for those who come after you. The intern you treat kindly today could be handling your company's merger tomorrow. I've lived long enough to discover that it's always good to err on the side of sending the text or forwarding an email if it means it might help connect someone you know with someone who needs it. Sixty seconds of your time could change someone's life, so make the effort. Being kind has a shelf life, and if your connections think of you as one of the good ones, all kinds of doors will be opened to you.

## CONNECT WITH THESE TAKEAWAYS

- Getting connected is easier than ever, but staying connected takes work.
- Know not only the "right" people but all people who deserve to be treated right.
- Remember the immortal words of Doug Ireland: "Nothing's impossible, Albert. Impossible just takes a couple extra phone calls."

## TEN

# THE LIKABLE

## CASE STUDY: THE LIKABLE UNICORN

Likability is synonymous with Jamie Kern Lima's brand. Likability helped her get crowned Miss Washington. It helped her stay longer than any other woman on the first season of *Big Brother*. And it contributed to Kern Lima's success as a TV news anchor. And it was as a news reporter and anchor that Kern Lima found her vocation. She'd always struggled with rosacea, and appearing on TV multiple times a day made the situation even more complicated. It was difficult for her to find makeup that would cover it without further irritating her skin. So she created her own. IT Cosmetics was born with Kern Lima's vision plus the expertise of dermatologists. IT didn't achieve success overnight, until it did. She spent two years sending her products to home shopping behemoth QVC in hopes of landing a spot, to no avail. But things changed when a producer found her at a tradeshow. The upbeat and charming Kern Lima persuaded the producer to try her eye cream, and suddenly she'd landed a ten-minute spot on QVC. The experience itself was terrifying, but Kern Lima persevered and developed an instantly relatable demo of her products. Wiping off her perfect face of makeup and exposing her red, rosacea-plagued skin, Kern Lima showcased the effectiveness of her products right there, in real time.

Putting her makeup back on showed how easy and effortless it was. When viewers saw this moment of vulnerability, they connected with a woman who they felt was just like them. On her first appearance, Kern Lima's entire inventory sold out. The company took off and, in 2017, Kern Lima sold it to L'Oréal for $1.2 billion. Since then, Kern Lima has become a philanthropist, mom, and author, devoted to helping people believe in and like themselves.

After running more than twenty-five hundred searches, I'm amazed at how often the candidate that prevails is simply defined by "plays well with others." Many companies end up having to fire (or wishing they could fire) a "brilliant jerk" on staff. But the Likable have the ability to stay employed and even get promoted simply through relational equity, a store of goodwill you've built up with another person over time. Learning to be likable is easier than you might imagine. This chapter will show you how to improve your likability. And with a crowded, noisy world, this trait may end up being more important than any other.

## WHAT WE KNOW

Imagine you have a big project coming up. It could be a presentation at work, or perhaps the task of researching, designing, and ordering uniforms for your kid's baseball team, or maybe it's a bathroom remodel. When assembling your team for this project, whom do you choose? The guy who knows the subject up and down, the expert in this area? Or someone less familiar with the material but who seems likable?

You might think this is a no-brainer, that of course it's the expert. Likability is one thing, but competency is another, more important thing. Indeed, when we're dealing with hypotheticals, most of us do say we'd go with the expert. But what happens in real life, researchers have found, is the opposite.

There was a terrific study done on this. Researchers discovered that the disparity between what we say we'd do versus what we actually do is a bit like when we self-report on our habits. Of course we read the newspaper, of course we recycle, we absolutely shop local! But in reality, we're not quite as virtuous as we think we are. Impulses and instincts take over, and we end up going with what we like rather than what we know is better.

The study uncovered two interesting things:

1. Feelings act as a gatekeeper; if you don't like a person, they won't have the chance to show their competency.
2. What little competency a person has will be maximized if they're liked; likability trumps competency almost every time.

Stay likable and the doors will be flung open wide. What's more, your likability will protect you from the consequences that may come with not being quite as competent.

## But I don't want to be a doormat

Being likable isn't the same as being a people pleaser. People pleasing comes from fear. Being likable comes from confidence. If you're worried about crossing over into people-pleasing territory on your journey to perfect your likability, don't be. As long as you have healthy self-esteem and your likability is an expression of your true self, you won't become a people pleaser.

It is possible, however, that you might be starting from a place of people pleasing. The psychological term for it is *sociotropy*. It's sometimes a symptom of anxiety or a product of past trauma. Moving from people pleasing to simply likable requires a lot more knowledge of psychiatry than I have. I'll simply say that, thankfully, sociotropy is rare. And I hope those stuck in a people-pleasing cycle will someday be able to come into the light of likability and enjoy the benefits that come with it.

As Unicorn Jared H. puts it, "Being likable doesn't mean you 'people please,' grinding away, saying yes to everyone. It means you take the time to invest in others, intentionally seek out relationships, and attempt to share in others' interests."

### *Does being popular count?*

Being popular is nice, and it certainly brings with it a lot of power and status, but it's not quite the same as being likable. A study published in *Current Directions in Psychological Science* (not exactly a "beach read" but fascinating in its own right) defined popularity versus likability. The popular were associated with social dominance, influence, and aggression. The Likable were emotionally well-adjusted and less aggressive. Popular people push and shove while the Likable welcome and unify.

**Likable fact:** the "beer question" has been used as a litmus test in US politics for decades now, but scholars say it's problematic at best. Thinking someone would be fun to be with at a bar or ball game is vastly different from thinking someone would be wise enough to handle the nuclear codes. In this case, when it comes down to it, you're going to want to go with the competent one over the likable one.

## WHAT WE'VE SEEN

Have you ever noticed that likable people really never talk about themselves but always turn the conversation toward you?

Again, there were lessons to be learned from my audience with President Clinton. Namely: focus the conversation on the other person.

Think about how this principle could help you in your professional life. In sales meetings, think how you can turn the conversation back toward the customer. In leadership situations, share stories and examples of other team members' wins. When you're speaking your vision for your organization's future, make it about everyone in the room.

### What's in a name? Maybe a job offer

It's classic Dale Carnegie: "Remember that a person's name is, to that person, the sweetest and most important sound in any language."

If you can make a person feel important by remembering—and saying—their name, you're well on your way to likable.

I try to be good with names, and usually I am, but I have a friend, we'll call him Larry, who makes a mission out of name recollection, particularly when dining out. I've seen it time and again. It's a feel-good moment for all involved. Showing respect to the server is the human thing to do *and* the likable thing to do. It helps remove the power dynamic of server and served. It makes issues easier to bring up and resolve.

Larry asks the server how long they've been working there. He'll find out where they're from, and if they're in college, he'll ask what their major is. When he goes back to that restaurant, he'll ask to sit in so-and-so's section whereupon he will follow up on anything he learned the last time—kids, graduation, nascent graphic design career, anything. (Larry has an uncanny ability to remember generations of servers at his favorite restaurants.) He takes genuine interest and is, I'm fairly sure, genuinely liked by waitstaff.

There's that great Muhammad Ali quote: "I don't trust anyone who's nice to me but rude to the waiter. Because they would treat me the same way if I were in that position." In recent times, observing how a person treats the server has become a litmus test for what kind of person you are. Dates are won or lost on it, and so are jobs. Think about that the next time you have lunch with your boss or a potential employer. Life is a "waiter test," and even if no one is watching, it's important to treat people with kindness.

## Go down to go up

Sometimes you have to hide your light under a bushel.

There's that famous story of Queen Catherine Parr, the last wife of King Henry VIII. Now, even those of us with very limited

European history knowledge know that it's bad news when you hear "wife" and "Henry VIII" in the same sentence. Henry had beheaded two of his previous wives by the time he married Catherine Parr. The story goes that Henry had deemed Catherine a heretic for her Protestant ideas and ordered her arrest (after which the execution would surely follow). Catherine found out, had a quick panic attack, picked herself up, and raced to Henry, explaining that any talk of Protestantism with him was just because she sought subjects that could keep Henry's mind off his ailing health. She was only a woman, after all, she added. As her husband, king, and intellectual superior, she submitted to his every word. He bought the story immediately, called off the arrest, and Catherine was back on Henry's likable list.

In Harper Lee's *To Kill a Mockingbird*, main character Scout's father, attorney Atticus Finch, is easily the smartest person in town. But he doesn't flaunt it. Instead, he is Maycomb's calm moral compass and tries to pass along these same values to his children.

"The one thing that doesn't abide by majority rule is a person's conscience," he tells Scout. In court, when he's cross-examining a witness for the prosecution, Atticus has plenty of "gotcha" opportunities like this one:

"About your writing with your left hand, are you ambidextrous, Mr. Ewell?" he asks.

"I most positively am not; I can use one hand good as the other. One hand good as the other," comes the response. Instead of spiking the ball in the end zone and explaining that this is exactly what ambidextrous means, Atticus keeps quiet and moves on.

For the Likable, knowing when not to talk is just as important as knowing when to talk. In my career, I have been in meetings with distinguished people, experts in their field, only to find that the least experienced person in the room has the most to say. No one knows more than them; they have it all figured out and aren't afraid to take your time telling you so. It's a testament to so many of my respected mentors' and colleagues' likability that they simply smile and let the person continue. I used to have a difficult time keeping myself from refuting these upstarts and reminding them just who they were talking to. But then I saw the masters at work, keeping quiet for the sake of saving the talker's pride, and by doing so, becoming all the more likable.

### Secondhand compliments are gold

Not talking has its merits as a tool for cultivating likability, but let me tell you what is a veritable flywheel of likability: secondhand compliments. Giving someone a compliment is a wonderful thing. It helps a person stand a little straighter and walk a little taller. But to supercharge a compliment, make it secondhand. Secondhand compliments are Batman to gossip's Joker. Same execution, different motivations. Secondhand compliments are when you tell someone something positive that another person told you about that person. For example, Nichole tells you that Jessica knocked the presentation out of the park, so you tell Jessica what Nichole said about her. This amplifies the good feelings Nichole has toward Jessica, engenders them from Jessica to you and from Jessica to Nichole. And you get to be at the warm and fuzzy center of it, sowing seeds of likability.

### Finding the Likable

I've always believed that the sooner you find out if a candidate is going to work, the better. No use wasting anyone's time. And likability is a great predictor of future success. As you've seen by now, the candidate-screening techniques I use here at Vanderbloemen are a bit . . . unorthodox. But I'm here to tell you it works.

## THE VANDERBLOEMEN LIKABILITY BAPTISM BY PARTY

A few years back, we were hiring for a VP of sales, and I strongly suspected we'd found the perfect candidate. It was December, so our Christmas party happened to be the day after our initial interview. I texted the candidate and asked if she'd like to come meet the team in this more festive setting. She responded quickly (another great sign!) and said of course. Well, she ended up being the life of the party. Sarah stayed till the very end, helping the crew that remained close down the venue and singing harmony for the Christmas carols that spontaneously erupted. The next day, those of us with clear enough heads excitedly texted about how much we liked the new VP of sales. She got the job, of course, and the rest is history.

### WHY HIRING MANAGERS LOVE THE LIKABLE

This is a bit tautological, isn't it? Although they may seem so at times, hiring managers are not automatons. When pricked they bleed, just like the rest of us. When a likable person crosses their path, hiring managers are as happy to like them as the rest of us are.

**Tips for cultivating likability at work:**

- Set aside a few minutes at the start of meetings to talk about something that has nothing to do with work.

- Coach your team on listening.
- Value empathy.

### Report from the Unicorns

Of our Unicorns, 5.72 percent reported likability as their strongest of the twelve traits. They can attest to the trust, grace, and opportunities that comes with being likable.

### Likable people are trusted people

"Because people like me, they are willing to listen and consider what I say," says Roy C. "Because folks like me and feel heard and included, it's often easier to get them to understand my way or process because they don't feel threatened by my response. My likability seems to allow people to relax their guard and think with a more open mind, knowing they can trust me to not criticize their views."

Gina B. vouches for the efficacy of remembering names and finds that the benefits of being likable are simply the by-products. "Knowing a person's name seems like a little thing, but remembering a name says to that person, 'You matter to me enough that I know who you are.' It is the first step in someone feeling cared for. Then, as we spend time together, I get to know their story. I listen because I am genuinely interested," she says. "It is simply a bonus that this interest reaps benefits relationally such as trust, loyalty, and grace."

## Being liked means getting more chances

"Results are important, but likability is more important," says Kristopher B. "If you get results but blow all your goodwill on the way, the second you make a mistake (and we all do!) people will pounce on you. Likability builds a goodwill bank that allows you to make mistakes with less risk."

Christopher J. has found likability to almost literally be a lifesaver. He says, "I am naturally curious and ask questions . . . then listen. Having been in the military and law enforcement, being effectively likable, asking questions and making connections has kept me and my teams out of harm's way more than I can count."

## Likability is an open door

Jeff H. shares that being likable has given him more opportunities faster. "I've always felt that being kind, likable, and genuinely friendly gets me where I want to go much quicker than if I weren't these things. I've gotten promoted faster thanks to being known as a good manager who is easy to work for."

### WHO IS LIKABLE? KEANU REEVES

Whether it's giving surprisingly profound answers on late night talk shows or going viral for the patience and care he takes with his fans, Keanu Reeves never seems to be anything but likable. Tales of his kindness and generosity fill the internet. He buys his stuntmen motorcycles. He takes pay cuts to get movies made. He takes public transportation and gives up his seat to ladies with bags. His girlfriend is age appropriate. He gives money to children's hospitals with as little recognition as possible. Keanu Reeves is one of the good ones or, more accurately, one of the excellent ones.

## WHAT WE DO

I know some of you might be thinking, with dread, "Oh great, now some tips for going out there and being the life of the party, interacting with people, and being so, so social." Some of you dread this because some of you are introverts. But listen, you know as well as anyone that introverts are very likable. Maybe even more likable than your average takes-up-all-the-air-in-the-room extrovert. You don't have to be everywhere, in front of everyone, to be a successful, likable introvert.

Albert Einstein, Eleanor Roosevelt, Abraham Lincoln, Rosa Parks, and Nelson Mandela were famous introverts. All were regarded as likable—at least by the majority of people. The minority here were not exactly on the right side of history. And think of famous present-day introvert (and Houstonian) Beyoncé. She rarely does interviews, she hates speaking in public, but you have to agree that she finds a way to connect with people, nevertheless. Our introverted likable Unicorns share how they make it work:

James W. says, "I am an introvert, but I function in a very public environment. Although it is energy draining, I convince myself to function in public spaces by capitalizing on my likability or charisma. I genuinely love people, so that is a tremendous help."

"I learned that people really like being asked about themselves, and they also feel connected if you have a story to tell that agrees with or restates what they have just said," says Abby M. "I am told that folks may agree or disagree with me, but they feel heard when they talk with me. And I also have people say that I cannot possibly be an introvert when I share that. This says to me that I have learned to function as an extrovert when I need to be."

Introverts can use other means of connection to make their likable presence felt. I knew a woman who would be all but invisible at public events but who would go home and write thoughtful emails to attendees, following up and establishing a friendly rapport.

Joshua K. learned to do something similar. "It wasn't easy or natural. But I started writing cards, remembering birthdays, sending encouraging texts, and learning to part with my time for the sake of meaningful conversations."

Social media is another great way to establish your likability without having to join the office kickball team or any other activity that requires too much social interaction. Thoughtful posts and shows of support for your friends builds likability fast.

### *Know what you're saying when you're not saying anything*

Introverts need to recharge after being in public or having long conversations with people. All of us need to learn similar self-knowledge when it comes to how we present ourselves.

Brad B. says, "It's important to lead with warmth. Have open body language, smile, make eye contact, and respect boundaries."

"From my facial responses to body language, people know that I am engaged with them," says Dave H.

## Care. A lot.

Empathy is an essential component of likability. Like the person who treats the waiter the same as she'd treat the CEO, genuine care for all people will make you liked and respected.

Scott W. has learned this from having worked all over the world. "Likability can be a skill to be developed," he tells us. "It can be authentic in every situation when you prioritize respect and empathy toward others, be they in a slum, palace, university, or coffeehouse."

"Be a servant," Leon G. urges. Boss, intern, coworker, we all need extra grace. "People struggle and are filled with overwhelming emotions. Make it your job to encourage, give hope, and always forgive."

"Care about people," says Kristi C. "That sounds so simple, but when you think about others, and genuinely care about their life, people want to be around you. In a work environment, this manifests in a more productive and effective group of people. This is because people want to do things for people they like."

Beltane G. reminds us of our shared humanity. No matter how much power a person has, no matter how confident they appear, "everyone wants you to genuinely show that they matter. All around us are hurting people who want to feel loved and accepted." If you can make others feel safe and bolstered, you'll be likable.

## Follow through

The second lesson I learned from my conversation with President Clinton is that timely, personalized follow-through is everything when it comes to likability. How many times have people made promises to you and haven't kept them? How many times has someone told you they'll follow up, only to forget? In my experience, people who actually follow through on what they say they're going to do, in a timely manner, are far rarer than you might expect. In my long-format interviews with more than thirty thousand individuals face-to-face, I've learned that follow-through is a rare trait among even the very best of the candidates we've interviewed.

## Stay humble

Humility is another key component of being likable. "Stay humble and others will like you," says Scott W. "But stay humble, strong, and rooted, and they will like *and* respect you."

James G. tries to keep his ego out of every situation: "My mentor always encouraged me to leave people better than I found them. When I walk into a room, it's never about me; it's about others. It should never be 'Here I am!' Instead, it's 'There you are!'"

## Ask questions

The unexamined life is going to find you less likable. Scott N. advises, "Observe carefully during interactions with people to gauge interest and communication. Ask open-ended questions. Ask them what experience or passion motivates them. Ask what they've learned from a failure or setback. Ask what their next step is to fulfill their dream. Ask them how you can help them get a win."

Asking questions doesn't have to be a serious, tedious task, however, as Kyle H. discovered. "In the military, I found out quickly that being a 'likable dude' carried nearly as much weight to the crew as being a good pilot. I worked on this quality by showing a serious interest in what other people liked. I asked questions, made jokes, and laughed with them, and I learned to smile a lot, even when I didn't feel like it. Most of all, I found being personable, uplifting, and encouraging had the greatest impact. As a result, when I was assigned to a trip, there would be a race to fill the rest of the spots on the crew."

Mike B. reminds us that asking questions doesn't apply only to people. "Have a thirst for knowledge that allows you to learn a little about a lot of things . . . which comes in handy when meeting new people and talking about life. Not only will it increase your relational capital in productive ways, it also allows you to control conversations and direct traffic to benefit people and groups."

## Do the work

It never hurts to invest a bit more time and energy in cultivating likability. Investments pay off.

"My greatest tip is to know a person's name and remember it," says David R. "Then, know at least two things about them, their spouse's name, children's names, occupation, anything. Just put in the effort to know something more about them. And smile!"

Dennis M. found that doing his homework made him much more likable. "I've had the opportunity to manage people from Germany, France, Brazil, Australia, China, and India. I took classes on different cultures so I could understand their motivations. This helped improve my likability and my managerial skills."

## Desperation never wins

While God may love a trier, as the saying goes, people generally don't. When you try too hard or look too desperate to be liked, it can be a real turnoff. When it comes to being likable, the best advice might just be to be yourself but a little bit better. Making small, thoughtful tweaks will always work better than a full-on offensive.

Take your time, make the effort, and you'll be more likable than ever before.

## LIKE THESE TAKEAWAYS!

- Stop talking. Listening will get you further.
- Remember, no matter what position we may hold in life, we're all people trying our best; act accordingly.
- Being likable is the foundation of relational equity and building a positive reputation for yourself.

## ELEVEN

# THE PRODUCTIVE

The movie *Enchanted* (What can I say? I've got daughters) stars a delightful Amy Adams as Giselle, a Disney princess thrust into modern-day New York City. She's confused. She's afraid. She's three-dimensional and no longer a cartoon. It's a really big change for her. She would have every reason in the world to curl up and cry. Instead, Giselle chooses to be productive. With a twist of her sash, a summoning of NYC-equivalent forest friends, and a song, she cleans the filthy apartment where she's taken refuge. "Ahhh," she sighs when the job is done. "Wasn't this fun?"

Being productive isn't always about fun, but it is about making the best use of your time and distinguishing yourself among the crowd. It's all too easy to kick projects down the road and let distractions get the best of you.

With the rise of social media, instant messaging, and an on-demand world, attention spans are falling like a stone. More time gets wasted than ever in the workplace. Conversely, when a productive person shows up to a job or task, they shine brighter than ever. In this chapter, I'll share my favorite productivity tips that have worked for me as well as some wisdom I've picked up from some of the most successful people I've interviewed over the years. Read on to learn the productive pathway to a new level of effectiveness.

## WHAT WE KNOW

Thanks to technology, we can work anytime and anywhere and with anyone. So why aren't we superproducers? The short answer is that we have too many distractions. You know how Henry David Thoreau was able to write *Walden*? He lived in the woods. He didn't have laundry to distract him. Or a phone. I joke, but it's partly true. Because we have access to anything, anybody, anywhere, it's harder for us to focus on the task at hand. This can be a reason working from home doesn't work out for everyone. Those who are successful at it are successful in part because they are able to focus on what they need to do without being distracted. Which is not to say that there's not plenty of—if not more—distractions in the office. Depending on who your coworkers are, you might be more productive at home because your cat doesn't stand in your office doorway and tell you real-time accounts of what happened on *House of the Dragon* last night.

There's not a one-size-fits-all prescription for productivity, but there are some key guidelines to follow. Being productive comes down to a few factors:

- knowing how you work best
- staying organized
- valuing outcomes over output

**Fun fact:** Harry S. Truman was fond of using the phrase "It's amazing what you can accomplish if you do not care who gets the credit." I think he got plenty of credit in his day, but can you imagine if what we know is only the tip of the iceberg?

### WHO IS PRODUCTIVE? MARTHA STEWART

Long before she became a household name, Martha Stewart was modeling, babysitting, and hustling her way through her teen years. She worked as a model through college and moonlit as a caterer after her stockbroking career. When an editor at Crown Publishing got to witness her catering ability firsthand, she quickly got a contract for a cookbook,

*Entertaining.* Her media empire took off from there. Stewart never stopped working, writing more cookbooks, hosting her own television shows, appearing on *Oprah* and later *Ellen*, and eventually starting a podcast with Snoop Dogg of all people. Even during her five-month prison sentence, Stewart worked and became a liaison between prison inmates and the authorities. Add to that multiple brand partnerships and guest appearances, commercials, and raising a daughter, and no one can deny that Martha Stewart is as productive as they come.

## WHAT WE'VE SEEN

You've got to know how to set yourself up for productive success. This comes down to letting your brain do what your brain does best, without distractions, and finding the right circumstances for that. If you have the option of working from home or not, it's important that you know which situation suits you better. When at work, keep track of your productivity during the day. Find out when it's highest and when you're in a slump. Plan accordingly.

### Staying on top of it all

Neuroscientist and author Tara Swart writes that reasoning, problem-solving, planning, and executing are functions of the brain that keep productive people going. She says these functions can stall or check out completely if you're faced with a repetitive, boring task, constant interruptions, or even an overly ambitious to-do list.

One of my favorite "productivity hacks" has to do with eliminating that kind of productivity-killing to-do list. It's actually more than a hundred years old. A gentleman by the name of Ivy Lee designed a method to maximize productivity for Charles Schwab's executive team by helping them focus on less in order to do more. It's simple and it works.

### THE IVY LEE METHOD

1. Step 1: Write down six of the most important things you'd like to get done that day.
2. Step 2: Order that list—for some it works best to do the smaller tasks first. For others, getting the big stuff out of the way first is more effective.
3. Step 3: Work through the list.
4. Step 4: Strike through the tasks you've completed. Everyone loves the dopamine that comes with crossing off a to-do list, right?
5. Step 5: Repeat.

Most of my team has their own system of to-do lists and productivity strategies that work for them. Apps, email reminders, pen and paper—it doesn't matter how you do it; the important thing is that you do it.

### Outcomes over output

I enjoy metrics as much as the next guy, and they certainly have their place, but measuring productivity in output is outdated. It worked when we were all in factories or on farms and new technology enabled us to do more with the same number of hours in the work-day. But it doesn't apply as nicely to the corporate world. (Even though much of the corporate world thinks it does.)

I interviewed a woman once who described a case of KPI (key performance indicator) overkill. The company where she worked was being badly mismanaged, so the owner hired two so-called management experts to come in and turn the company around. To give you an idea of the brain power here, one of the pair had come out of retirement and didn't know how social media worked. The woman I was interviewing was duly respectful of her last position but noted that the Toyota Production System didn't work as well for her sales and marketing team as it did for the manufacturing floor. Nevertheless, she was tasked with making every part of her job into a metric.

She had all the spreadsheets and numbers and data, but ulti-mately what really mattered, she thought, were the outcomes, not the output. She could make X number of website improvements per week, bring in Y leads, and decrease ad spend by Z percent, but what wasn't tracked or valued were the sales or how they were made. She was told to keep updating her spreadsheets and not waste "unproductive" time looking for better ways of communicating to leads or investigating what was working or what wasn't by A/B testing digital ads. There's not a lot of room for creativity, discov-ery, or innovation when output is being tracked. When outcomes are the concern, however, then true, meaningful productivity can happen.

## Report from the Unicorns

Our survey revealed 5.72 percent of respondents who said they were prominently productive. Not surprisingly, they were also the respondents who gave the most robust answers and had the most productivity tips to offer.

## PRODUCTIVE PARENTING PERSPECTIVE

One trend we've discovered is that (no shock) becoming a parent kicks your productivity into overdrive.

Amanda B. says, "The biggest mindset shift for me when it came to productivity was when we had kids. I realized I could spend excess hours at work, being super distracted, and investing my time in things that didn't matter. Or I could laser in on the most important work, dedicate blocks of time to cranking through projects, and prioritize my energy, which freed up more time to spend with my kids and family."

"While I'd like to think I have always been productive, becoming a mother made me even more productive," says Kathy C. "To balance my time and get things done, I find the best, most efficient way to work. Due to multiple time commitments, work needs to be completed in the allotted time."

## GETTING THINGS DONE AND EARNING RESPECT

Jamie G. says, "I have learned time and energy management. I only have so many minutes in the day to produce. I don't like spending time on *things*. I like investing my time in producing results. If I ever feel 'busy,' I back up and evaluate. I would rather be productive."

Stephanie R. says her productivity helps with job security: "Over the years I have often been told that it takes more than one person to replace me in any given position. I can get done in four hours what it takes most people six to eight hours to do. I am an achiever with a high sense of responsibility and like to see results."

Jennifer J. says that her productivity helped her earn her boss's respect and trust. "In my current role, I spent the first eighteen months working in a different city from the rest of my team—and my boss. It was important to me to demonstrate that this work arrangement could be successful," she says. "I was also creating an entirely new department in the organization, building a team from almost scratch, and developing a plan for the next two years. I started setting two-month stretch goals and sharing them with my boss; every two months I emailed him the previous report with an update on every project (ideally just one word: completed) and my goals for the next two months. I also shared those additional projects that weren't on my goal list but which I accomplished. This served a couple of purposes: it made sure he knew everything I was contributing and getting done despite the distance, but it also kept me accountable for moving forward and allowed him to speak into my strategy if he felt it was off course. Four years later I'm on-site with my team but still do this report six times a year. My boss has told me several times how helpful it is to him."

Marlene A. says her productivity makes her trusted by her supervisors. "I try to be very efficient with my time," she says. "I have a system to my day that involves answering every email and phone call, as well as categorizing and prioritizing emails so I know what to tackle first. My days often get hijacked with other projects, but I still make my communication with others a priority. My supervisors know that if they give me a project and a timeline, they can count on me to get it done well and on time."

**WHY HIRING MANAGERS LOVE THE PRODUCTIVE**

Productivity can be tracked, and every manager knows that what gets measured makes the whole team look good.

**Tips for cultivating productivity at work:**

- Lessen the grasp. This might sound counterintuitive, but studies show that workers are more productive when they are working on their own terms and on a more flexible schedule.

- Don't reward productivity with the next project. If a team member completes a task and exceeds expectations, reward that person with time or kudos, not more work.

- Demonstrate responsible time management.

- Show respect for everyone's time by keeping meetings on task and short.

## WHAT WE DO

Unicorns are not only productive; they know the best ways to become productive.

### Have daily, achievable goals

Brett R. says to find the best to-do list for you. "I've learned to create detailed to-do lists that are categorized and prioritized," he says. "While I use a number of digital systems for this, I have found that having to physically write it out on index cards helps me process each task and remember them as well. I also display the index card on my desk so I can see what I need to accomplish each day. I focus on one task at a time until it's complete then move on to the next one. I have found that multitasking (with most tasks) actually is less effective because my focus is divided, and I'll end up not giving it my best mental effort."

Angela S. says trust in the lists. "Making lists has been my MO since I can remember! No matter if it is a to-do list, pros and cons list, or grocery list—if I want to be productive, I have to have goals and dates to reach or (hopefully) exceed those goals. It's easy to get caught up in busy work and forget the projects and tasks that are productive to my job, my boss, and my church. My motto is, 'Keep the main thing the main thing.'"

Terry L. says no matter how you set your goals and keep focused, organization is key. "One of the biggest ways that I improved my productivity was by being organized. By knowing what was on my calendar for a particular day, I was never blindsided or unprepared," he says.

He also has a good technique for staying focused during meetings: "I never take a laptop to a meeting, lest I become distracted. It is always a pen and a notebook. I also try not to overcommit myself by carefully spacing my meetings out during the day. I am far from perfect, but have found that this works well to keep me on track and producing the high results that I am known for."

## Know yourself

Mason P. says knowing how you work is crucial to unlocking your productivity potential. "To maintain productivity I think one of the best tips is to recognize the rhythms of your work and regularly evaluate how the season determines the rhythm," he says. "By dynamically adjusting how much time you're going to spend on an initiative based on the current season's constraints, you can maintain and even increase productivity. Additionally, evaluating effectiveness regularly is important for quality production, as it is not really productive if that simply means 'busy.'"

*Try as many strategies as you need to!*

Victorine M. tells us: "Some years back, I was absolutely terrible with productivity habits at work. Whenever I set a goal, I failed to accomplish it because I always found excuses to procrastinate. I thought productivity wasn't something for me. Something had to change, and that put me on a journey of research, self-discovery, and ultimately, a life-changing obsession with productivity. I dove deep into how successful people did it. I made a list of more than fifty productivity tips and tricks, going through them and noting what didn't work for me. I kept what worked and that changed my life. I am now proud to call myself a productive person, a problem-solver, and a solution to the challenges around me and the world at large. I have accomplished goals I never thought possible."

Victorine M. shares some practical ways she stays productive:

1. Write down the three most important tasks every day.
2. Eliminate distractions.
3. Stop multitasking.
4. Stop being a perfectionist.
5. Wake up earlier.
6. Exercise.
7. Have meaningful goals to pursue.
8. Stop doing everything yourself.
9. Reduce the number of meetings to attend.

## PRODUCTIVE TAKEAWAYS!

- There's a difference between productive and busy. Learn it.
- Everyone has different productivity hacks. Try them all and find what works for you.
- Track your productivity. This is great for year-end reviews and work-related conversations but also for your own learning on what works best for you.
- Singing a happy working song helps with productivity. Just make sure your colleagues/forest friends are on board with it.

# TWELVE

# THE PURPOSE DRIVEN

## CASE STUDY: THE PURPOSE-DRIVEN UNICORN

"I don't feel like I've achieved what I wanted to achieve yet, even though every day I get an email from another girl who tells me the difference that Girls Who Code has made in her life," says Reshma Saujani. "I'm not done yet." Saujani is the daughter of refugees and grew up with gratitude for the opportunities the United States gave her family. She says this instilled in her an early drive to give back and inspired her passion for public service. Saujani's purpose in creating Girls Who Code was to empower women and girls to go after the same opportunities—and salaries—as men. Seeing the lack of women in tech positions, stemming from the lack of girls in coding classes, Saujani was driven to do something about it. "If our American women are going to work to put food on the table and pay for the mortgage, then we better make sure that they get put into jobs that pay well and that pay their worth. That's why I'm such a huge advocate about computing jobs, because those are the jobs," she says.

Saujani is a living example of how the American Dream can be for anyone. She's passionate about making room for everyone—immigrants, women, youth. She believes that diversity is the key to innovation and problem-solving. Because of this, for Saujani, more women in tech just makes sense: "I think that if we want to cure cancer, we have to teach girls

to code. If we want to do something about climate change,

we have to teach girls to code. If we want to solve homeless-

ness in our city and our country, teach girls to code. They're

change makers."

Everyone who has joined our company has taken a pay cut to do so. And our company keeps winning awards for "Best Place to Work" and "Top Company Culture." Why? People come for our cause, and we hire people who are themselves driven by a well-defined cause that supersedes money. Developing your sense of "why" will accelerate the "what" that you do. This chapter will help you develop your sense of "why" and project it to those around you in a way that makes them winning and irreplaceable.

## WHAT WE KNOW

In 2018 the world was riveted by the story of twelve Thai boys and their soccer coach who had gotten trapped in a cave at a national park. The cave flooded unexpectedly, and when authorities arrived at the entrance and saw the boys' bikes and shoes, they knew something had gone wrong. Within hours the Thai Navy SEALs were deployed; within days the world had come to help.

The Thai cave rescue was one of those rare situations in which the purpose was indisputably clear: rescue the boys. There was no gray area, no political misgivings. Countries rushed to the aid of the Thai authorities. Volunteer cave rescue divers arrived from England. For eighteen days, more than ten thousand purpose-driven people from all around the globe did what they could to support the rescue effort. Locals cooked and did laundry for the volunteers; nearby farmers agreed to have their fields flooded and crops ruined for the sake of diverting water from the cave. Classmates of the boys held vigils, prayed, and made a thousand paper cranes. Dozens of governmental agencies sent aid, top water engineers from Bangkok, and ultimately one hundred volunteer divers, who were on the scene to assist with the miraculous rescue of all thirteen people.

The official in charge of the rescue mission was Narongsak Osatanakorn. At the end of the mission, he told reporters, "The mission was successful because we had power. The power of love. Everybody sent it to the thirteen."

If love isn't the highest of purposes, I don't know what is.

### Everyday purposes

Events like the Tham Luang cave rescue are, thank God, rare. But you don't need a disaster on a global scale to be purpose driven. Common, everyday goals drive the Purpose Driven; the only difference is that these goals add up to more than the sum of their parts.

Unicorns know that professional success depends on two things:

1. You have a strong sense of purpose.
2. You find an organization whose purpose aligns with yours.

Think for a moment what having a sense of purpose can do for a person. This is something Cornell professor Anthony L. Burrow has been studying for much of his academic career. There are real benefits to having a purpose, chief of these being that people with purpose tend to live longer. But what actually is behind this statistic? Burrow found that having a purpose helps people stay psychologically stable. In a study, he found that people with purpose reacted with more equanimity to both positive and negative situations.

### The Purpose Driven at work

McKinsey did a deep dive on purpose in the workplace post-pandemic. They found that COVID-19 caused an estimated two-thirds of workers to reevaluate their purpose at work and in life. (Hello, Great Resignation.) This was ultimately a good thing, however, as it forced both individuals and organizations to uncover and define what their purpose was. The best result of the Great Resignation was a sort of corporate game of fruit basket upset, where people dashed away from one job and found a place where their purpose matched the company's.

The McKinsey research found that when employees feel that their purpose is aligned with the organization's purpose, benefits include "stronger employee engagement, heightened loyalty, and a greater willingness to recommend the company to others." When you have a purpose and when you find an organization that shares that purpose, both you and your employer benefit.

**Fun fact:** *Thirteen Lives* is the 2022 Ron Howard film based on the Tham Luang cave rescue. Viggo Mortensen and Colin

Farrell play the British cave divers who first find the trapped boys. Mortensen told *Variety* that the film depicted "a great example of the way things can be when people think in a good way, as opposed to the way most people—certainly politicians—think nowadays."

## WHAT WE'VE SEEN

The Vanderbloemen vision is to serve teams with a greater purpose by aligning their people solutions for growth: hiring, compensation, succession, culture, and consulting. Among our clients, we've worked with more than fifty Christian denominations, knowing that each has unique beliefs and needs. Therefore, when I'm hiring, I look for candidates whose purpose aligns with ours. We've had to pass on otherwise ideal candidates who lacked the respect for all faiths that we value here at Vanderbloemen.

This is why it's so important to be purpose driven, both as an organization and as an individual. A clearly defined why can save a lot of time and heartbreak. Have you ever hired a marketing agency for your organization? If you have, I'd be willing to bet that the first thing they propose is defining your mission, vision, and values. Why? It's not necessarily just to get $150,000 and an eight-hour catered discovery session. Agencies that do it right realize that when executed well and defined correctly, your mission, vision, and values will inform every decision your business makes. These give you your purpose, which is your company's touchstone.

*Report from the Unicorns*

Of survey respondents, 11.3 percent say that they're dominantly purpose driven. For them, being purpose driven is a way of life.

### SHARPENS FOCUS AND DECISIONS

Deb S. says she'd always lived with purpose but that an injury forced her to really narrow down her purpose. "I have always been goal driven. I learned to be more effective by being curious, setting clear priorities for my time, and building margin into my schedule. I learned to set priorities on my time when an eye injury forced me to slow down. After two eye surgeries in six weeks, my physical vision was reduced. I simply could not do my job the same way. I learned to do only those things that moved the program forward and met the needs of those I served. My whole life became more focused—no pun intended—as I gave up reading most of my emails and planned to do the hardest tasks during my peak hours. The benefits are still revealing themselves in the form of less internal stress, clearer communication within the team, and greater effectiveness."

Adam J. agrees in the power of purpose, saying, "Knowing the motivation of why you work and keeping it at the forefront of your mind each day eventually changes the way you make decisions, prioritize, manage time; it even impacts emotional responses to work like resiliency and satisfaction."

"I have learned to focus on the principles, not the personalities," says Greg M.

Unicorn Joe M.: "I had a mentor who really helped me get a grasp on what purpose driven is. He told me to always search for the why. It has kept me, and my teams, on task. If you can't answer the why, clearly you shouldn't do it."

## PURPOSE REVITALIZES

Roy R. says being purpose driven helps give life to projects. "Knowing the why truly makes what you do more effective with better benefits; though it brings challenges, it also brings growth and knowledge. We had a program that was seeing declining participation, year after year. By looking at the actual purpose of the program, we were able to look at it a different way and to better communicate with the people we wanted to reach. We saw more enthusiasm for it within our organization as well as with those who would participate in the program."

## HELPS OTHERS

"I have been called a subject matter expert in diversity/inclusion and executive management," says Marcus H. "Through my career, I have impacted the lives of over ten thousand youth and families through programs in organizations I have served as president and CEO. My passion led me to a place where I could make a positive difference for a lot of people."

"It took me a while to discover my purpose, and even after discovering it, I was not intentional in living it," says Rudy L. "It took a few more years, after facing a health scare that could have ended my life, that I finally gained the confidence to pursue it at all costs. I finally started living my purpose. I became more satisfied with my life, and my results were magnified. My actions have directly benefited thousands of people across the globe."

## WHY HIRING MANAGERS LOVE THE PURPOSE DRIVEN

Knowing your personal purpose and knowing your company's purpose are the first steps to finding if you're the best fit for the position. Making sure these are compatible early on will save your hiring manager and company time, energy, and money.

**Tips for cultivating a purpose-driven workplace:**

· Have absolute clarity in your mission.

· Understand what motivates you and what motivates your team.

· Celebrate when you "catch" team members living the purpose.

## WHO IS PURPOSE DRIVEN? LEYMAH GBOWEE

Gbowee was a young mom in Liberia, West Africa, when she ended a civil war that had ravaged her country for fourteen years. The brutal civil war was between the president (dictator, really), Charles Taylor, and tribal warlords. Thousands of people had been killed, maimed, and raped, their homes burned, their children forced to be soldiers, their infrastructure and security in ruins. One night, Gbowee had a dream in which God told her to "gather the women and pray!" So she did. Gbowee rallied women in her Lutheran church and then across the country, ordinary Christian and Muslim women who wanted better for themselves and their children. They participated in nonviolent protests for months, including sitting in a field across from the executive residence.

Taylor finally agreed to meet with the women and promised that he would attend peace talks. When the peace talks stalled, Gbowee and the hundreds of women who had been peacefully watching from outside the hotel marched to the entrance of the room where the men were meeting. As the men tried to leave, without an agreement, Gbowee announced that the women would not allow the men to leave until a peace agreement had been reached. Within days the peace agreement was complete and on August 18, 2003, the Liberian Civil War ended. In 2011, Gbowee was awarded the Nobel Peace Prize.

## WHAT WE DO

At each meeting we have at Vanderbloemen, we start by connecting with our vision and discuss where we've seen our values at work in the past week. This is a great opportunity for me to share how our purpose is witnessed by others. I'll tell my team about an encounter at the golf course or when I was out to dinner. Almost always, I'll have met someone who has heard of us and our phenomenal team. This tells me our purpose is preceding us. Then we check in with a "consultant on the road." One of our consultants will Zoom in and give us an update on a client they've been working with. They'll discuss various VanderValues that the client shares with us and other positive news. And then, one of our in-office teammates will stand up and tell us about a coworker who put a VanderValue into action that week. From the world to our office, our purpose is at work.

### You can't fake purpose

To be purpose driven, it's essential that you know yourself well enough to know your passions and interests. It's hard to become purpose driven externally. It's actually impossible. Purpose comes from within.

If you're not quite sure of your exact purpose, it can be helpful to look to your leaders. Standout Willie M. writes, "Finding someone who models the purpose-driven life has helped me tremendously." If you can't completely articulate your purpose yet, observe people you admire, try their purposes on for size, and I assure you, you'll find what you're about—or not about—quickly enough.

### Ask yourself why

Unicorns are all about asking why. I had so many examples of this, it was hard to select just a few. Here are some of my favorites.

Robert M. says, "I feel that if you don't know why you're doing something, then you are just being busy. My role as leader is to make sure people know the why, the purpose, so that momentum is built, the vision is central, and the goals are accomplished."

"Being able to answer the why question brings clarity to exactly what I should be doing," says Tom I. "As a leader, it helps me clearly articulate to my organization as well. I've gotten better at this by consistently asking the why question over and over again for every decision we make as a team."

Danese C. says, "The why is what pushes me to excel in all the other areas. If there is not a why or a purpose, all is meaningless. True fulfillment is in the why."

"I learned early on that we are not guaranteed any amount of time," says William B. "Therefore, we do not need to spend our time majoring in the minors. We do not need to spend our time focusing on what is but a mere distraction. We need to know why we exist—why we are, why we are here, what our purpose is—and then we need to organize and work together to accomplish our why."

### Distill it and drill it

Once you have your purpose, hold onto it, and keep it front of mind. Distill your purpose into as few words as possible and then drill it home at every opportunity.

Unicorns are very clear on their purpose. One survey respondent, Brian M., tells us, "I created my personal vision and values. I read over this weekly to keep myself in tune."

Another Brian M. tells us that his purpose serves as an indicator for how well he is communicating: "It has been important for me to simplify my purpose and my team's purpose as much as possible so that it can be remembered and shared with others effectively. I've boiled my purpose down into two words. This helps bring the why to new team members quickly and clearly. Because it's been simplified to two words, I can use it as a gauge by asking my team members what we do. If they answer with the two words, then they understand. If they cannot reply with those two words, then I know I need to do a better job at explaining what our purpose is to others. This clarity has had the single biggest impact in my leadership and on my team."

### Check in with your purpose regularly

Standout Gary R. says, "I daily remind myself of my why. I do this progressing from a generalized sense of purpose to my unique, specific purpose. This centers my mind and my soul and refocuses my goals for the day. It helps me stop the purposeless daydreaming, which creatives are notorious for, and instead helps me envision the best ways to meet my purpose."

### Let your purpose do the work

Even if it's plastered on Post-it Notes and on your letterhead—heck, maybe even your forehead—actively checking in with your purpose is essential. When your purpose is a touchstone, decisions will fall into place. Standout Andrew M. shared with me some early experience he had with letting purpose do the heavy lifting. His leader taught him and his team to "never put on events or do certain activities for the sake of doing them or because 'that's how we've always done things.' Instead, we were to keep in mind our why. With that at the forefront, we intentionally planned services, events, retreats, and small groups. As a result, our team was unified, and our organization was thriving."

Years later, Andrew M. says he still uses this technique. "I have carried those lessons with me into the role I have served in since that time, with similar success. It goes to show that purpose-driven leadership is a fundamental component of effective teams. In short, having the proper perspective keeps us on task and on target."

"Being purpose driven is what motivates me to work on and become better in the other eleven attributes," says Brian L. "Being fast, authentic, agile, a solver, an anticipator, prepared, self-aware, curious, connected, likable, and productive are all skills that help me to be more effective in my core purpose. For me, purpose driven is what inspires all the rest."

More than 11 percent of respondents said they were primarily purpose driven. And it's no wonder. You can't be a Unicorn without knowing exactly what your purpose is. Purpose is what gives you that passion for using the rest of your Unicorn traits, weaker though they may be, to become your true Unicorn self.

## PURPOSE-DRIVEN TAKEAWAYS!

- Find your why and try to find a workplace that aligns with it. That's it. The rest will fall into place.

## CONCLUSION

# WHAT'S NEXT?

At the very upper end of the island of Manhattan, there's a museum called The Cloisters that houses the Metropolitan Museum's medieval art and architecture collection. One of the biggest draws to The Cloisters is its Unicorn Tapestries. These are a series of intricately woven wall hangings made at the turn of the sixteenth century depicting, you guessed it, a unicorn and its capture. Although his story is fraught with hunting dogs, people clamoring for a grasp of his magical horn, and his actual death, the final panel shows the restored-to-life unicorn seemingly content in his new position, wearing an expensive brocade collar and sitting idyllically under a fruit tree. People wanted this unicorn. People sought out this unicorn. Now, the unicorn sits in a place of honor, celebrated and valued by people who know how special he is.

I hope this book helps you find just such a place.

I have a phrase I use a lot at work: "If you've seen one client, you've seen one." What I mean by that is that no nonprofit, church, or any other organization that we've ever worked with has been the same. I've never been able to say, "Oh, this client is kind of like this other client we worked with two years ago; we can assume it will go the same way," because that has never happened. Each organization is different.

We can't predict the challenges that await us, but we can be ready for them. Develop and grow these twelve traits, and I can assure you that you will be more than ready: you'll be a leader, a sage, and a visionary. You'll be a Unicorn.

# ACKNOWLEDGMENTS

There are far too many people involved in this project for one name to be on the cover.

This could never have happened without the tireless efforts of the team at Vanderbloemen. Since its inception fifteen years ago, people have come together to try and help our clients go further and faster by providing people solutions. Perhaps the biggest talent solution of any organization is finding the right team members. We have now interviewed more than thirty thousand top-level candidates, and the data we have gathered over the years was the genesis of this book.

But an idea and data can only provide the beginning of a book. Tim Burgard of HarperCollins has been a champion of this work long before others knew of it and a delight to work with. The creative and marketing team at Vanderbloemen worked tirelessly to help this become a reality. My agent, Esther Fedorkevich, was a cheerleader and ambassador of this idea even before others believed in it. And perhaps more than anyone else involved in the project, my colleague and contributor Elizabeth Paulson put feet to the vision. This book would not have come to be without her genius and hard work.

Finally, I thank my wife, Adrienne. Aside from questionable taste in men, she's simply the best. Thanks for setting the tone and pace for everything that Vanderbloemen has achieved. Thanks most of all for calling great efforts and work out of me that I didn't realize were there. You are the original and best version of the Unicorn I've ever known, and I'm honored to do life and work alongside you.

# INDEX

# ABOUT THE AUTHOR

**WILLIAM VANDERBLOEMEN** is founder and CEO of Vanderbloemen Search Group. In 2008, William combined more than fifteen years of experience as a senior pastor with the best practices of executive search to forge a brand-new industry: executive search for values- and faith-based organizations. The firm is known worldwide for excellence in identifying talent and values matches for teams and has been recognized with numerous awards: *Forbes Magazine* named it as one of the best small businesses in the country. *Entrepreneur* magazine named Vanderbloemen as the best company culture in the country. Vanderbloemen has studied data gathered over the last fifteen years and lessons learned in three thousand searches to determine what habits the very best candidates exhibit and how others can learn those habits. He lives in Houston with his wife, Adrienne, their seven children, and Pearl, their standard poodle.